Jesus, the Suffering Servant of Mark and Isaiah

A Role Model for Christian Discipleship in the Namibian Church

Thorsten Prill
Misseline Gordon

Bibliographic information published by the German National Library:

The German National Library lists this publication in the National Bibliography; detailed bibliographic data are available on the Internet at http://dnb.dnb.de.

ISBN: 9783346501868
This book is also available as an ebook.

Cover image: wikipedia.org

© GRIN Publishing GmbH
Nymphenburger Straße 86
80636 München

Print and binding: Books on Demand GmbH, Norderstedt, Germany
Printed on acid-free paper from responsible sources.

The present work has been carefully prepared. Nevertheless, authors and publishers do not incur liability for the correctness of information, notes, links and advice as well as any printing errors.

GRIN web shop: https://www.grin.com/document/1140397

Jesus, the Suffering Servant of Mark and Isaiah

A Role Model for Christian Discipleship in the Namibian Church

Misseline V. Gordon

Namibian Theological Research Papers

Volume 4

Series Editor: Thorsten Prill

Dedication

I dedicate this book to my grandmother, Elizabeth Bock, an example of servant leadership, to my family and friends who supported and prayed for me, and finally, to all students and staff members of the Namibia Evangelical Theological Seminary.

Acknowledgements

I am very grateful to Rev Daan van der Kraan (The Netherlands), Dr De Wet Strauss (Namibia), Dr Jan Parker (England) and Dr Thorsten Prill (Scotland) for their helpful comments and corrections.

Windhoek, September 2021
Misseline Gordon

Contents

Foreword   1

Introduction   2

Chapter One: Mark's Portrayal of the Servant   4

Chapter Two: The Two Faces of Suffering   23

Chapter Three: Christological Images   33

Chapter Four: Christian Discipleship   43

Chapter Five: Mark's Model of Discipleship and the Namibian Church   53

Bibliography   61

Foreword

While some scholars reject the notion that the evangelist Mark portrays Jesus as the *Suffering Servant* of Isaiah, Misseline Gordon, who lectures at Namibia Evangelical Theological Seminary (NETS), holds that this is exactly what he does. Having convincingly argued her case, she demonstrates that the concept of the *Suffering Servant* provides a helpful model for both Christian discipleship and leadership. If Christian discipleship means following Jesus and the goal of leadership is to help Christians to do so, disciples of Jesus will need to embrace the biblical message that sacrifice, suffering and service to others constitute essential elements of the Christian life. In a country like Namibia, such an understanding challenges not only cultural conventions and theological views but also church practices and leadership patterns. For example, respect for leaders, as Misseline Gordon points out, is an important traditional Namibian value. However, it is problematic when Namibian church leaders insist having a special status in society and, thus, a right to privileges. Such an attitude is in stark contrast to the sacrificial servant-leadership of Jesus which we can see in Mark's gospel. The same is true for the claims of the prosperity gospel that Christian discipleship and leadership are first and foremost about success, wealth and power. Gordon's research paper encourages not only Namibian readers but the wider church to return to the Scriptures and discover the true nature of Christian discipleship.

Thorsten Prill
Edinburgh, September 2021

Introduction

In his Gospel, Mark presents Jesus as fulfilling the Old Testament image of the *Servant of God* which is found principally in the later chapters of Isaiah. Thus, in chapter 1, verse 14 Mark speaks of Jesus as the one who brings good news (cf. Isaiah 52:7). In verse 2 of the same chapter, he mentions that Jesus' way is prepared for him by John the Baptist (cf. Isaiah 40:3f.). In verse 10 he tells his readers that the Spirit comes on Jesus at his baptism (cf. Isaiah 61:1). However, Mark presents Jesus not simply as the Servant of God but as the servant who fulfils his divine mission through suffering. At least, this is the impression one can get from texts like, 'For even the Son of Man did not come to be served, but to serve, and to give his life as a ransom for many' (10:45). In this verse, an echo can be heard from Isaiah 53:4-5 where the prophet declares, 'Surely he took up our pain and bore our suffering […] But he was pierced for our transgressions; he was crushed for our iniquities.'

Throughout his gospel, Mark's focus is on the deeds of Jesus rather than his teachings. Mark particularly emphasises the themes of service, sacrifice and sovereignty. He presents Jesus, as Norman Geisler (2007:71) writes, 'as an ideal Levite, servant of man and God, before the altar and on the altar.' At first sight, it seems as if Jesus' suffering only starts in Gethsemane where he isolated himself with three of his closest disciples to spend time in prayer. We are told by Mark that Jesus was 'deeply distressed and troubled' (14:33) and that he disclosed to Peter, James and John his emotional state by saying 'My soul is overwhelmed with sorrow to the point of death' (:34). However, a careful reading of Mark's gospel shows that the theme of suffering is introduced much earlier in the gospel. In chapter 8, verse 31, for example, Jesus tells his disciples 'that the Son of Man must suffer many things and be rejected by the elders, the chief priests and the teachers of the law, and that he must be killed and after three days rise again.' This announcement is repeated in chapter 9, verse 31 where says to them, 'The Son of Man is going to be delivered into the hands of men. They will kill him, and after three days he will rise.' The third prediction of his suffering and death can be found chapter 10. Here Jesus lets his followers know that he will soon be mocked, spit on, flogged and killed in Jerusalem (:34).

While some scholars such as D. E. Nineham (1986) are critical of the view that Mark portrayed Jesus as the Servant of Isaiah 44-55, I will show that this is what Mark did and that the concept of the suffering servant provides a helpful model for discipleship, a model that is essential for the contemporary Namibian church. In chapter 1, we will explore scholars such as Peter. W. Smuts, James R. Edwards and Paul Barnett who among many others support the idea that Mark portrays Jesus as Isaiah's suffering servant. Subsequently, I will attempt to identify citations and allusions used by Mark to portray Jesus as the suffering servant. Thereafter an explanation will be given of these citations and allusions. Furthermore, in chapter 2, I will establish a connection between Mark and Isaiah 40-55 by an in-depth exploration of the four so-called servant songs of Isaiah, which will help us to determine the role of the servant. Besides determining the role of the servant, I will also seek to clarify the purpose of the servant's suffering. Chapter 3 deals with the Christological images in Mark and how they relate to the image of the suffering servant. In chapter 4 I will examine how Jesus' suffering can be a model for his disciples. In the last chapter, I will explore how this model can be applied to the Namibian Church of today.

Chapter One

Mark's Portrayal of the Servant

The opening verse of Mark's Gospel 'The beginning of the gospel about Jesus Christ, the Son of God' (Mk 1:1), sets the tone for the whole book. The meaning of the good news about Jesus Christ, the Son of God provides broad scope for the deeds of Jesus and his ministry. However, it is also the heart of Mark's Gospel. Just as a heart functions to pump blood through the veins of a body and keep it alive, Jesus Christ, the Son of God, gives life to those who believe in him. Therefore, we want to examine whether Mark's Jesus is indeed the one who gives eternal life and how he does that. Mark introduces his Gospel as the good news about Jesus Christ the Son of God. Being the Son of God signifies a greater meaning. Could it be that this meaning has its origin in Isaiah's suffering servant?

To explore the true meaning and significance of Mark's portrayal of Jesus as the suffering servant in Isaiah, we will do a primary exploration of the views of three scholars (i.e., P.W. Smuts, J. R. Edwards and P. Barnett) on this matter. Do they also see that as part of his Christology Mark makes use of the servant image from Isaiah? If so, what part does Mark use? And how does he use the servant image of Isaiah in this part? In the second part of this chapter, we are going to investigate if there are any imagery links to the suffering servant of Isaiah in the Gospel of Mark. Firstly, we will look at direct citations used by Mark. Secondly, we will further look for texts that might be allusions to, or examples from, Isaiah 40-55.

Three Scholarly Views

Peter Smuts (2013:6) points out that Mark identifies Jesus both as the Christ, i.e., the Messiah, and the Son of God (cf. 1:1, 1:11; 5:7; 9:7; 15:39). The quotations which follow the opening verse of chapter 1 and which introduce John the Baptist to us are from the Old Testament books of Malachi and Isaiah. Mark 1:3 is a direct quote from Isaiah 40:3. However, the phrase 'for our God' in Isaiah 40:3 becomes 'for him' in

Mark 3:1. According to Smuts, the prophet Isaiah prophesied centuries ago about Jesus' future coming. Jesus' arrival was of such impact that Isaiah speaks of a forerunner who had to prepare the way for him. Mark reveals that John the Baptist was this forerunner, the one who came to prepare the way for the Lord (1:4).

Furthermore, Smuts (2013:114) holds that Mark 8:27-38 'represents a significant turning point in Mark's Gospel, where the narrative shifts to Jesus' death and resurrection.' He explains that the focus of this passage lies in Jesus' identity. It was not until Peter confesses Jesus to be the Christ (Mk 8:29b), that Jesus, in response, begins to speak about the suffering, rejection, death and resurrection of the Son of Man (8:31). Smuts goes on to suggest that this self-designated title *Son of Man* has its roots in Daniel's vision in Daniel 7:13-14. There, Daniel sees 'one like a son of man coming with the clouds of heaven' (2013:13). Smuts considers that Jesus' self-designated title as Son of Man in Mark's Gospel (8:31; 13:26; 14:62) refers to this same triumphant figure in Daniel 7. However, he also considers that in the context of Mark 8:31, Jesus connects the titles 'Christ' and 'Son of Man' with the Suffering Servant of Isaiah 53:3 (:114). Smuts suggests that Jesus' revelation that *'Son of Man must suffer much and be rejected'* (Mark 8:31), shows he was reflecting on the Old Testament Scriptures that are alluded to in Mark 9:12; 14:21a. It was his knowledge of the Old Testament which caused him to connect the titles of 'Christ' and 'Son of Man' with the Suffering Servant of Isaiah 53:5-6; 12b (:114). Thus, Smuts implies that Jesus' use of *Son of Man* does involve the imagery link of the Suffering Servant of Isaiah 53:5-6; 12b (:114).

James Edwards (2002:284) argues that Jesus' second passion prediction, 'The Son of Man is going to be betrayed into the hands of men' (Mark 9:31), already 'reflects the language of the Servant of Yahweh in Isaiah 53:6, 12 (LXX).' Edwards suggests that this verse indicates that Jesus will die for the sins of others (:284). According to Edwards, Mark indicates that the Christian faith finds its meaning essentially in the death of Christ. For Christ did not die for his sins (he was sinless) but for the sins of those at whose hands he died (:283-284). That the Son of Man is going to die for the benefit of the sinful world, according to God's will, Edwards argues, is reminiscent of Isaiah 53:6, 12. In other words, Edwards holds that Mark uses the concept of the Suffering Servant of Yahweh and applies it to Jesus.

Lastly, Paul Barnett (1991:198) believes that Jesus' statement in Mark 10:45, 'for even the Son of Man did not come to be served, but to serve, and to give his life as a ransom for many', confirms that he saw himself as the suffering servant of Isaiah 53:1-12. Barnett asks the questions 'How did the Son of Man serve?' and '[B]y what action was he slave to all?' In Mark 10:45b Jesus stresses that his coming was 'to give his life as a ransom for many'. Barnett points out that Jesus taught his disciples about his impending suffering, rejection and death on three occasions (8:31-32; 9:31; 10:32-34), but without explaining why he 'must die' (8:31) (:198-199). It is only here in 10:45b and 14:24 that Jesus gives a reason for his death: his death would be 'for many'. Barnett concludes that

> [t]he background for these words in Mark's Gospel is Isaiah's poem of the suffering servant in Isaiah 52:13-53:12 where the word "many" occurs several times: '[…] my righteous servant will justify many, and he will bear their iniquities […] For he bore the sin of many and made intercession for the transgressors (Isaiah 53:11b-12) (:198-199).

Jesus' teaching regarding his impending suffering and death is found in Mark 8:31; 9:31; 10:33. What Mark implies with the passion predictions parallels the understanding that the servant will suffer and die 'for many' as indicated by Barnett. Therefore, Jesus' suffering and death should be understood in light of the suffering servant in Isaiah 52:13-53:12. Neither can Jesus' suffering and death be separated from who he is, i.e., the Christ and the Son of God (Mark 1:1, 11; 15:39). It is because of his Sonship and Messiahship that he had to suffer in accordance with God's will, even unto death (cf. Isaiah 53:11-12). To get a better understanding of Jesus' Sonship and Messiahship, we will now explore how Mark uses Isaiah in his portrayal of Jesus as the *suffering servant-messiah*.

Imagery links of the Suffering Servant of Isaiah in the Gospel of Mark

Since the imagery of the suffering servant derives from the so-called 'Servant Songs' in Isaiah 40-55, I will now look at connections between Mark's Gospel and these chapters of Isaiah and other related chapters or verses in Isaiah. First, we will consider texts that are regarded to be direct citations by Mark of verses from chapters 40-55. The purpose is to see whether Mark quotes from these chapters to portray Jesus as the Suffering Servant. The texts that will be discussed in this section are Mark1:3 (Isaiah 40:3), Mark1:11 (Isaiah 42:1), Mark 14:24 (Isaiah 53:11d-12) and Mark 10:45 (Isaiah 53:11d-12c). I will then examine some other texts in Mark's Gospel that are or might be alluding to Isaiah 40-55. These texts are Mark 2:7 (Isaiah 43:25), Mark 8:31 (Isaiah 53:3a- 4a, 10a, 11a-12a), and Mark 14:60-61; 15:4-5 (Isaiah 53:6-7).

The Call for Preparation

'A voice of one calling in the desert, prepare the way for the Lord,
make straight paths for him.' (Mark 1:3)
'A voice of one calling: In the desert prepare the way for the Lord,
make straight in the wilderness a highway for our God.' (Isaiah 40:3)

Isaiah 40:1-3 refer to the end of Israel's exile in Babylon. These verses call for the preparation of the way for Yahweh's return to his people. In the second half of the quotation in verse 3, Mark uses the LXX version of Isaiah 40:3 almost word by word, except, as mentioned before, where Isaiah makes use of the phrase 'for our God' Mark writes 'for him'. James Brook (1991:39-40) comments, 'In Isaiah "the Lord" was God, but in Mark it is Jesus.' Thus, in his introduction of his Gospel, Mark already sheds light on Jesus: it is the gospel about Jesus Christ, the Son of God (Mark1:1). Mark's alteration of the text from 'our God' to 'for him' shifts the focus to Jesus, who was known in the early church as 'the Lord'. In other words, 'the evangelist is already pointing to Jesus' and as a result, identifying Jesus with God' (Watts 2007:113-114). The messenger of whom Isaiah speaks, Mark identifies as John the Baptist: 'And so John came [...] and this was his message: After me will come One more powerful than I' (Mark 1:4a; 7a). Mark identifies John with the forerunner who would prepare the way for the Lord. He did not see himself worthy to untie the thongs of the Lord's sandals (Mark 1:7), because his message was all about the one to come. His message was all about the one who was more powerful than the messenger.

The Voice from Heaven

'And a voice came from heaven: You are my Son, whom I love; with you I am well pleased.' (Mark 1:11)
'Here is my servant, whom I uphold, my chosen one in whom I delight; I will put my Spirit on him, and he will bring justice to the nations.' (Isaiah 42:1)

In Mark's Gospel, Jesus' first appearance on the scene was when he came from his hometown Nazareth to John the Baptist to be publicly introduced to Israel through his baptism. What is imperative here is the voice of God speaking from heaven. First heaven was torn open, and the Spirit descended on him like a dove. Then the voice spoke from heaven 'You are my Son, whom I love: with you I am well pleased' (1:11). In Isaiah 42:1, a similar voice is heard from heaven is speaking 'Here is my servant...my chosen one in whom I delight; I will put my Spirit on him.' As a matter of fact, the voice from heaven and its declaration in Mark 1:11 alludes to several Old Testament passages, as Larry Hurtado (1998:19-20) notes:

'You are my Son' echoes Psalm 2:7, a psalm originally addressed to the ancient Jewish kings. 'A son whom I love' echoes Genesis 22:2, where God addresses Abraham, telling him to offer his son [...]'With you I am well pleased' reflects Isaiah 42:1, where God points to his servant as one chosen to speak for him.

In contrast to Hurtado, Alan Cole (1999:109) sees verse 11 as a combination of only two verses, Psalm 2:7 and Isaiah 42:1. While the first one deals with the Messiah the second one focuses on the suffering Servant. Cole continues to argue that the merger of these two concepts is a perfect expression of the twofold nature of

Jesus' work. He explains: 'The Greek word *agapētos*, translated beloved, has also the nuance of 'only' when applied to a child, and so was particularly appropriate here. The other word son in Greek, *pais*, can mean son and 'servant', so would have been doubly appropriate when describing Jesus […] (:109)' Geoffrey Cogan (1995) considers why both concepts need to be brought together. He writes: 'So many in Israel saw no real connection between the Messiah and the Servant. Here the voice of God from heaven unites them. Jesus was God's Christ, but he would endure profound suffering in the course of his mission for his Father' (:30)

Christopher Wright (2005:106-107) holds that 'the echo of Isaiah 42:1 'My loved one, in whom I delight' is the opening verse of a series of songs in Isaiah 40-55 about One called the servant of the Lord.' He explains that the verse starts by introducing the servant like a king, but as the servant song develops it becomes clear that the servant will accomplish his calling not by kingly power, but through suffering, rejection and death (:106-107). The second servant song (42:1-4; 5-9) introduces the servant and also gives a job description of the servant (in chapter 2 I will deal in detail with the description of the servant).

Eduard Schweizer (1970:39-40) on the other hand suggests, 'It is what God does for Jesus that gives him his unique position.' He further says that 'the heavenly voice and the designation of Jesus as the Son God is what matters' (:40) The second half of the verse of Mark 1:11, 'with you I am well pleased', was a type of formula that resembles the choosing of a prophet (Ps 2:7) (:40). The significance of the voice of God, both in Isaiah and Mark, serves to indicate the similarity of the unique position of the Servant of the Lord in Isaiah and Jesus as the Son of God in Mark.

To conclude, the announcement God made in Isaiah 42:1 'Here is my servant, whom I uphold, my chosen one in whom I delight' and the divine declaration in Mark 1:11 'You are my Son, whom I love; with you I am well pleased' cannot be treated as two unrelated statements. On the contrary, the first announcement must be seen as a prophecy about the coming suffering-servant-messiah that the second announcement declares to be fulfilled, or as Donald English (1996:40) puts it: 'The voice from heaven, also apocalyptic in character, despite lengthy scholarly discussion, still seems best understood as bringing together insights from Isaiah 42:1.'

Poured Out for Many

'This is my blood of the covenant, which is poured out for many, he said to them.' (Mark 14:24)

'By his knowledge my righteous servant will justify many and he will bear their iniquities.' (Isaiah 53:11d)

'Therefore, I will give him a portion among the great, and he will divide the spoils with the strong, because he poured out his life unto death [...] for he bore the sin of many.' (53:12)

In chapter 14, verses 2 to 25, the evangelist tells his readers about the origin of the Lord's Supper, still an integral part of Christian life and worship today. Jesus took the bread and the cup of Passover wine in his hand and explained the significance of what was about to happen on a cross outside Jerusalem. He gave the two elements of the traditional Passover meal a new meaning: they would represent his body and blood. Hurtado (1998:36) notes: 'So, the cup represents the death of Jesus, which is interpreted as happening on behalf of others (for many) and as being the sacrificial blood/death that institutes a new covenant. To share this cup is to include oneself in the many (v. 24) for whom Jesus died.' The words of verse 24 echo the words of both Isaiah 53:11 'my righteous servant will justify many' and Isaiah 53:12 'he poured out his life unto death [...] For he bore the sin of many'. Raymond Ortlund (2005:359) points out that Jesus' death on the cross was not a defeat but a divine strategy. Commenting on Isaiah 53:11-12 he writes: 'Isaiah's prophetic eye can see that Jesus was taking the initiative by his death, making the will of God prosper in the most improbable way imaginable. At his cross Jesus achieved the ancient purpose of God with victorious love' (:359).

Wright (2005:155-156) notes that 'the essence is clearly that Jesus referred to the shedding of his own blood as a covenantal act and that it is for the benefit of others.' Several Old Testament passages seem to be combined in Mark 14:24. Thus Wright states that '[t]he blood of covenant recalls Exodus 24, but the new covenant is from Jer.31:31-34, which was promised by God for his people and included complete forgiveness of sin.' When Jesus made the declaration in Mark 14:24, he clearly saw himself as the servant figure and interpreted his earthly mission and especially his suffering and death on a Roman cross in terms of Isaiah 53 (:156).

William Lane (2010:507), who shares Wright's view, writes that verse 24 not only alludes to Exodus 24:6-8, which speaks of the ratification of the Sinai covenant by the sprinkling of sacrificial animal blood, but also evokes Jeremiah 31:31-33 where we read about God's promise to replace the old covenant, which was broken by his people, with a new covenant in the last days (:507). Lane continues:

> That promise is now sealed through Jesus' action and the death it antici-
> pates. The saying over the cup directs attention to Jesus as the one who
> fulfils the divine will to enter into covenant fellowship with his people on a
> new and enduring basis. The latter part of the saying explains the vicarious
> character of Jesus' death in terms of Isa. 53:12 [...] (:507).

Similarly, Edwards (2002:426) argues that 'the phrase 'poured out for many' becomes reality not in the wine of the upper room but in Jesus' death on the cross of Golgotha. He points out that in Mark 10:45 a similar formulation can be found when Jesus confirms that the purpose of the 'Son of Man is to give his life as a ransom for many.' Edwards furthermore stresses that 'many' is not a limited select group, but that this term alludes to all those who benefit from the suffering of Isaiah's servant of chapter 53, verse 12 (:427). In other words, the phrase 'many' for whom the Son of God poured out his life unto death includes both Jews and Gentiles. Walter Wessel (1984:761) comments: '"Many" here means "all", as Calvin clearly recognized: "By the word many he means not a part of the world only, but the whole human race."' This inclusive, universal character of Jesus' sacrificial death is hinted at in passages, such as Isaiah 42:6b which speaks of the servant-Messiah as the one who will be made 'a covenant for the people and a light to the Gentiles' and Isaiah 49:6b where the servant is promised to be made 'a light for the Gentiles' who will bring God's 'salvation to the ends of the earth'.

Ransom for Many

'For even the Son of Man did not come to be served, but to serve, and to give his life as a ransom for many.' (Mark 10:45)
'By his knowledge my righteous servant will justify many and he will bear their iniquities [...] because he poured out his life unto death [...] For he bore the sin of many.' (Isaiah 53:11b-12c, e)

In Mark 1:38 Jesus says to his first disciples 'Let us go somewhere else – to the nearby villages – so that I can preach there also. That is why I have come.' Jesus' words demonstrate that preaching the good news of God's kingdom was significant to his mission (cf. English 1996:61). Jesus came from God to preach good news. However, it is here in chapter 10, verse 45, that for the first time in Mark's Gospel Jesus reveals the motive and ultimate purpose of his coming to earth: 'to serve and not to be served, and to give his life as a ransom for many.' Jesus' suffering and death were the ways in which he would demonstrate his servanthood. Wessel 1984:721) notes 'that the entire phrase "to give his life as a ransom for many" emphasizes the substitutionary element in Jesus' death.' In other words, verse 45 unveils not only the motive and purpose of Jesus' mission but also the basis of human salvation. The word 'ransom' was a widely used economic term (Hurtado 1998:172). It was the price paid to release a prisoner, slave or forfeited piece of land. Consequently, Jesus' death became the price he paid on behalf of humankind for their liberation from the slavery of sin. Having said that, verse 45 together with verses 42 to 44 also reveal an important aspect of Christian discipleship, as David Hewitt (1995:146) points out: 'Jesus turns the value system of the world totally upside down. The life of discipleship is to be marked with humility and service, and the supreme example of this is Jesus himself, who is about to give his life for them.'

The second part of 10:45 correlates with the imagery language found in Isaiah 53:11b-12c, where the servant of God is pictured as the one who bears the sins of others by dying in their place. Jesus uses this picture from Isaiah to explain the meaning of his Messiahship. He sees his own suffering and death in the light of the

Servant Songs. This seems to be the position of authors like Geoffrey Grogan (1995:140), Alan Cole (1999:244) or William Lane (2010). The latter writes:

> The majestic figure of the Son of Man is linked here with the community which will be vindicated and saved in the eschatological judgment because Jesus goes to his death innocently, voluntarily and in accordance with the will of God. This corresponds perfectly with the main thought of Isa. 53 (:384)

However, not all the scholars see such a link between the suffering servant of Isaiah 53 and the passion of Jesus as we find it recorded in Mark's Gospel, and particularly in Mark 10:45. Among those scholars are C. K. Barret and M.D. Hooker who have questioned the idea that the words of verse 45 are an echo of Isaiah 53. Hence, I will explore and evaluate their views in more detail. First, I will look at the reasons why Barret and Hooker reject the view that Mark 10:45 has its background in Isaiah 53. Thereafter, I will devote my attention to those scholars who hold the view that there is a connection between Mark 10:45 and Isaiah 53:11-12. The aim will be to see how these scholars evaluate the arguments of the critics like Hooker, Barret and others. Finally, I will present my own conclusions.

According to Hooker (1991:247-251), almost all commentators assume that Mark 10:45 is based on Isaiah 53. However, the question in the debate is whether Jesus sees himself as the suffering servant of Isaiah 53. Hooker's first objection is that the keyword 'serve' (*diakoneō*), that many scholars assume presents a link, is absent in Isaiah 53 or rather in the LXX. Furthermore, she argues that *diakoneō* conveys the meaning of domestic service in the New Testament. Hooker's second objection is that the early church tradition behind Mark 10:45 could not have identified Jesus with the Suffering Servant of Isaiah 53 because the Servant is the servant of Yahweh and not a servant for many. Thus, she suggests that the servant of Isaiah 53 exclusively serves God and not his people. However, Hooker agrees that the LXX speaks of someone 'who serves many' in Isaiah 53:11, 'though it is a variation of the Hebrew'. Hooker holds that the only word that is common in Isaiah 53 and Mark 10:45 is the phrase 'many'. Her next argument is based on the comparison of the phrases 'the Son of Man', which we find in Mark 10:45, and 'the one like a Son of Man' which is used in Daniel 7. Hooker stresses that Mark's 'Son of Man' is the one who gives his life, whereas in Daniel 7 it is others who die and 'the one like a Son of Man' is presented as the victorious ruler. Thus, in Hooker's opinion *diakoneō* which means 'to serve' in the context of Mark 10:45 is in contrast with the ruling Son of Man in Daniel 7. Finally, Hooker argues that the word 'ransom' (*lytron*) in Mark 10:45b, does not occur in the LXX of Isaiah 53, and that *lytron* in Mark 10:45 does not correspond with *asam* ('sin offering') in Isaiah 53:10. Having looked at Hooker's objections, I am now going to examine those arguments that defend a connection between Mark 10:45 and Isaiah 53.

Rikki Watts (2007:203) argues that the background of Mark 10:45 is to be sought in Isaiah chapter 53. He explains that the keyword *diakoneō* which we find in the first half of Mark 10:45, 'For even the Son of Man did not come to be served but to serve', is an often-used term in the New Testament and that it occurs less frequently in the Old Testament. While Hooker bases some of her arguments on the claim that *diakoneō* is absent in the LXX, Watts suggests that *diakoneō* only appears at a later stage. Consequently, it should not come as a surprise that it cannot be found in Daniel 7. Furthermore, he argues that the terms servant (*diakonos*) used in Mark 10, verse 43 and slave (*doulos*) used in verse 44 do not signify a different meaning from the word *diakoneō* in verse 45. Jesus has already indicated in his use of the terms that they are in parallel with one another, i.e., that their meaning is synonymous. The nouns 'slave' and 'servant' suggest a similar idea as the verb 'to serve'. Service, ransom, and 'for many' echo the same idea and language of Isaiah 53:11-12. All these words stress the act of giving which is exactly what the suffering of the servant entails: to give himself willingly. Watts continues to describe Paul's use of *diakoneō* as inseparable from his understanding that he, Paul, is a slave (*doulos*) for Christ. Consequently, Watts suggests that Paul sees himself as being Christ's *doulos*, and that it is for the benefit of others. Hence, it is not inappropriate that the servant also serves the many as suggested in Isaiah 53:11. Finally, Watts deals with Hooker's objection that the Son of Man in Daniel 7 is a ruling figure. Watts points out that Mark's Son of Man is not without authority, because he gives his life as a ransom, it is taken from him. Similarly, Kim Huat Tan (2016:145) notes that both in Isaiah 53:11 and Mark 10:45 the ideas of 'service' and 'giving up of the life' are closely connected. While the phrase used in Mark 10:45 is *diakoneō*, the term used in the LXX of Isaiah 53:11 is *douleuō*. Tan's explanation is worth quoting in full:

> But behind the LXX stands the Hebrew word *'ābad*. It must be insisted that *diakoneō* is a legitimate translation of the Hebrew *'ābad*, and it is often used and understood as a synonym *douleuō*, the LXX term. Hence it is precarious to mount an objection based on the difference in Greek terminology, especially when the two terms are legitimate translations of the Hebrew. Moreover, in Mark 10:44 the term *doulos* (the noun) is found and is used as a synonym of *diakonos* in v. 43. Once the synonymous nature of the two terms is accepted, we may legitimately see a parallel between Mark 10:45 and Isaiah LXX (:145).

Tan continues to point out that the phrase 'to give one's life' in Mark 10:45 semantically resembles the Hebrew in Isaiah 53:12, which speaks of pouring out one's life (:145). He adds that the Greek word for many (*pollōn*) reminds us of the Hebrew word *rabbîm* of Isaiah 53:11-12: 'The Servant dies for many who would be the beneficiaries of his self-giving.' Finally, Tan recognises Hooker's objection that the LXX does not translate the Hebrew word *asam* with the Greek word *lytron*, but he believes that this does not present us with an unsolvable problem. Thus, he writes: 'But if we think of Mark 10:45 as not meaning to be a translation of Isa 53:10, but a summary and a creative appropriation of the task of the Servant in that passage, the force of this objection will be ameliorated' (:145).

The same point is made by Sydney Page (1992:660) who writes that 'both texts Mark 10:45 and Isaiah 53 combine the ideas of servanthood and atoning death. They also present the servant who voluntarily gives his life as a ransom for many. The Greek *lytron* meaning 'ransom' carries the same meaning as the Hebrew *asam* 'guilt offering' in Isaiah 53:10. Again both texts suggest that what is given is given for many. Both texts, when speaking of 'many', refer to those who benefit from the servant's death.

According to R.T. France (2002:402), there are two problems with Hooker's and other scholars' criticism. Firstly, they do not give enough attention to the larger Markan context, and secondly, they fail 'to recognize that Mark 10:45 is not a translation of Isaiah. 53:10-12, but rather Jesus' interpretative summary statement thereof as it concerns his mission' (:402). Craig Evans (2002:120-121) notes that the language might be absent, but the imagery concept of the suffering servant is present in both Mark's Gospel and Isaiah's four servant songs, of which Isaiah 53 is the climax, that points to the future suffering of Jesus.

This prompts the question, does Jesus see himself as the suffering servant of Isaiah 53? In my view, Mark has been influenced by the framework of Isaiah 40-55. He makes a connection with the passage of Isaiah 52:13-53:12. In Mark's gospel, Jesus identifies himself as the servant of Isaiah 42:1. We can see that in his reaction which is recorded in Mark 9:12, 'Why then was it written that Son of Man must suffer much and be rejected?' Jesus knows that he is the Son of God, and that he is the fulfilment of the suffering servant of Isaiah 53. The intimate father-son relationship in Mark, chapter 1, verses 1 and 11 testifies to Jesus' foreknowledge and the ransom saying in Mark 10:45 confirms his knowledge. As said before, Isaiah 53:10 and 12 allude to Mark 10:45. The words 'ransom' and 'guilt offering' both have the same meaning. *Lytron* which means 'ransom' carries the same meaning as the Hebrew *asam* which describes a 'guilt offering' in Isaiah 53:10. Both these texts suggest that the ransom and the guilt offering are 'for many', and both refer to the same servant who gave his life for the benefit of others. In addition, the covenant affirmation in Mark 14:27 'this is my blood of the covenant that is poured out for many is' alludes to the words of Isaiah 53:12 'he poured out his life unto death'. All these parallels and imagery links in Mark's Gospel and Isaiah 40-55 show that Jesus interpreted his death in the light of the servant songs, but more prominently in the light of Isaiah 53.

I will now continue to explore those texts in Mark's gospel that are or might be allusions to Isaiah 40-55. These texts are Mark 2:7 (Isaiah 43:25), Mark 8:31(Isaiah 53:3a- 4a, 10a, 11a-12a) and Mark 14:60-61; 15:4-5 (Isaiah 53:6-7).

Allusions that Portray Jesus as Isaiah's Servant of Yahweh

In the following section, we will have a closer look at some of the texts from Mark's gospel that might contain allusions to Isaiah 40-55. Some of these texts might be clearer than others.

Who Can Forgive Sins But God Alone?

'Jesus said [...] Son your sins are forgiven.' (Mark 2:5b)
'Why does this fellow talk like this? He's blaspheming! Who can forgive sins but God alone?' (Mark 2:7).
'I, even I, am he who blots out your transgressions, for my own sake, and remembers your sins no more.' (Isaiah 43:25)

The context of these texts from Mark chapter 2 is the healing of a paralytic man. Four men brought a paralysed man for Jesus to heal him. Jesus acknowledged their faith and declared the sins of the sick man to be forgiven. This enraged the teachers of the law who were present, and they began to condemn Jesus. Victor Babajide Cole (2006:1176) comments: 'They objected in their minds to the possibility of any mere mortal presuming to forgive sins, regarding the claim to be able to do so as blasphemous, since only God can forgive sins [...]'. In their eyes, Jesus assumes an authority that belongs only to God and by doing so he is insulting God. In fact, this was the very charge that became the basis on which Jesus was later sentenced to death (Mark 14:61-64). The scribes here strictly adhere to the Old Testament teaching that only God himself has the authority to forgive human sins – an authority, as Lane (2010:95) points out, that was never attributed to the Messiah. The latter 'would exterminate the godless in Israel, crush demonic power and protect his people from the reign of sin', but never forgive any sin. The religious teachers clearly see themselves as the ones who need to defend God's honour against the suggestion that a human being can do what is exclusively God's privilege (Hurtado 1998:36). Barnett (1991:46) suggests that Jesus' words point to the future, i.e., "they are prophetic of the time after his death and resurrection when all those who put their faith in him will be forgiven and receive salvation".

The notion that God is the one who forgives sins can also be found in Isaiah. Thus, in Isaiah 43:25, God says to Israel, 'I, even I, am he who blots out your transgressions, for my own sake, and remembers your sins no more'. This is an impressive declaration for at least two reasons. Firstly, despite Israel's failure to obey God he has decided to pardon his people (Nsiku 2006:839). Secondly, God claims that he is the only one who can forgive human sins, i.e., to blot out their transgressions. Allan Harman (2005:305) gives some helpful insight into the meaning of the phrases 'to blot out' and 'to remember no more':

> The verb for 'blot out' (Heb. *mocheh*, part.) is used at times in the Old Testament in connection with God's judgement (blotting out the memory of Amalek, Exod. 17:14; blotting out the name of the unrepentant, Deut. 29:20). But it also appears in passages like this which are speaking of salvation [...]. 'Transgressions' and 'sins' are used in parallel, while 'blot out' is paralleled with 'not remember'. To say that God 'will not remember' sin is equivalent to saying that he will forget it. While the verb is simply 'he will not remember', yet the addition of words such as 'no more' (NIV) in English translation are certainly warranted because of the synonym 'blot out' and also the general context.

At this point we need to ask the question, does Jesus have the authority to forgive sin or is he committing blasphemy as accused by the teachers of the law? Jesus' ministry as portrayed in Mark 1:1-8:29 reaches a climax with Peter's confession 'You are the Christ' (8:29), which is followed by another important declaration in Mark 10:45, 'For even the Son of Man did not come to be served, but to serve and give his life as a ransom for many.' However, the first time we encounter the term 'Son of Man' is here in chapter 2, verse 10. The self-descriptive designation 'Son of Man', which Jesus uses, could, as English (1996:67) notes, simply mean 'this man'. This is its characteristic meaning in Old Testament passages, such as Psalm 8:4 and Ezekiel 2:1. However, the term Son of Man strikingly resembles the phrase 'one like a Son of Man' in Daniel 7. Both designations hold eschatological significance. Mark's Son of Man will be exalted, just as the Son of Man in Daniel 7. He will sit at the right hand of the Mighty One and will return on the clouds of heaven

(Daniel 7:13; Mark 14:62). English comments that '[i]n this confrontation about the extent of his authority over sin and disease such a reference would be appropriate, though we must not assume that everyone present would immediately perceive the total significance [...]' (:67).

Although Jesus prefers the term Son of Man that does not make him less than God or to be without divine authority. Thus, Mark tells us that at his baptism and transfiguration God publicly declares that Jesus is his Son (Mark 1:11; 9:7). Jesus' sonship is later confirmed by his crucifixion (Blombeg 1997:351), when a Roman centurion states, 'Surely this man was the Son of God' (15:39).

Wright (2005:150) argues that there are three broad categories of the Son of Man saying. The first category includes all sayings where Jesus speaks about his earthly ministry. Jesus uses the term to assure the people that he has authority over human sin, sickness and nature (Mark 2:10, 28). The second category concerns his suffering, rejection and death (Mark 8:31; 9:31), while the third category of the Son of Man sayings, which is the largest of the three, consists of sayings that talk about Jesus' future return in glory (Mark 14:62). Wright continues to say:

> Taken together, these three categories are remarkably comprehensive as a way of encapsulating how Jesus saw his own identity as well as how he envisaged his immediate and long-term destiny. He was the one, firstly entrusted with authority in ministry, which he exercised over sin, disease, death, nature and even such fundamental ordinances of the Law as the sabbath. It was a startling and unique authority which raised eyebrows, questions and hackles all around him. But as he exercised that 'unauthorized authority', it led him into conflict with the existing authorities. That conflict eventually engineered his rejection and death [...] However, beyond suffering and death lay the vindication of resurrection and the exercise of heavenly authority (:150-151).

Although the term Son of Man is absent in Isaiah, the servant's vindication and exaltation both in Isaiah 52:13, 'See my servant will act wisely; he will be raised and lifted up and highly exalted' and Isaiah 53:12, 'Therefore I will give him a portion among the great, and he will divide the spoils with the strong, because he poured out his life unto death [...]', ultimately point us to the eschatological authority of the Son of Man described in Mark 10:45; 14:62; 2:7. J.A. Motyer's comment on Isaiah 52:13 is particularly helpful. He writes:

> The Lord here promised action on behalf of his people in which he would be personally present, and this was followed by his personal coming to Zion (8) after he had bared his arm in salvation (10). It is in the Servant that the Lord fulfils these promises. *Act wisely* [...] combines wisdom and effectiveness; the wisdom of true prudence, not in the weak sense of caution but in the true sense of knowing exactly what to do in order to bring about the intended result [...] The threefold exaltation (*raised ... lifted up ... highly exalted*) expresses a dignity beyond what any other merits or receives and is surely intended as a clue leading to the identity of the Servant. It is impossible not to be reminded of the resurrection, ascension and heavenly exaltedness of the Lord Jesus (1999:424).

Jesus as Son of Man had the authority to exercise the forgiveness of sin during his earthly ministry because he was equally God (Isaiah 43:25).

Rejected by Men

'He then began to teach them that the Son of Man must suffer many things and be rejected by the elders, chief priest and teachers of the law, and that he must be killed and after three days rise again.' (Mark 8:31)

'He was despised and rejected by men, a man of sorrows and familiar with suffering [...] Surely he took up our infirmities and carried our sorrows [...] Yet it was the Lord's will to crush him and cause him to suffer [...] after the suffering of his soul he will see the light of life and be satisfied [...]' (Isaiah 53:3a, 4a, 11a-12a).

Jesus neither accepts nor denies that he is the Messiah as declared by Peter in Mark 8:29. Instead, he introduces a new teaching that the 'Son of Man must suffer many things and be rejected by the Jewish authorities and that he must be killed, and after three days rise again' (Mark 8:31). These teachings of suffering, rejection and death, will eventually become the theme that dominates the rest of Mark's Gospel.

In these teachings, Jesus uses a different title, namely 'Son of Man'. This self-designation will be discussed in greater detail at a later point. However, it is worth noting, in Jewish-Aramaic writings, as Lane (1974:294) points out 'the idiom sometimes functioned as a circumlocution for 'I'''. From this, the assumption can be made that Jesus referred to himself when he used the phrase. In the same sentence, Jesus announced that he would also be rejected. This prompts the question, 'Who would want to reject the Son of Man?' Was it godless and wicked? Those who had no or little contact or interaction with him? This would be a plausible answer. But how shocking it must have been to hear from Jesus that he would be rejected by the Jewish authorities. The assumption here clearly is that the Jewish leaders (Mark 8:31) and all humanity are guilty (Mark 9:13) for rejecting Jesus. In Isaiah, it was the nation of Israel who despised and rejected the servant. This rejection was part of his sufferings. We do find that the prophecies of Jesus' passion reflect an identification of the Son of Man with the suffering servant in Isaiah 52:13-53:12. As Lane (1974:300-301) puts it, if the phrase 'suffer many things' is an allusion to Isaiah 53:4, 11, then it is equivalent to 'bear the sins of many' (cf. Mark 10:45). This brings us to the last text that might be an allusion to Isaiah 53.

He Did Not Open His Mouth

'Then the high priest stood up before them and asked Jesus, are you not going to answer? [...] But Jesus remained silent and gave no answer.' (Mark 14:61)

'The chief priest accused him of many things. So, again Pilate asked him, Aren't you going to answer? See how many things they are accusing you of. But Jesus still made no reply, and Pilate was amazed.' (Mark 15:3-5)

'He was oppressed and afflicted, yet he did not open his mouth: He was led like a lamb to the slaughter, and as a sheep before Her shearers is silent, so did he not open his mouth.' (Isaiah 53:7)

Jesus was arrested and brought before the Sanhedrin. During his night trial, false accusations were made against him. Amid all these false accusations, Jesus, however, remained silent. He did not defend himself. John Grassmick (1985:183) suggests that the silence of Jesus frustrated the court because they could not proceed as planned. Considering the hour that the trial was conducted, Jesus' silence might have made them uncomfortable, because they did not act according to the regulations of the Sadducees (Schweizer 1970:322-323). The night meeting was not an official meeting, otherwise, there would have been no need for the morning meeting.

Ben Witherington (2001:384) suggests that if the Jewish leaders had acted by themselves, they would have stoned Jesus more privately, but they wanted to put an end to the Jesus movement. Therefore, they needed to involve the Romans, who represented the state of law. At the handing over of Jesus to Pontius Pilate, the Roman procurator who interrogated Jesus at the second trial, Jesus made no reply. His attitude is remarkably like the attitude of the servant as Isaiah describes it, 'the servant was oppressed and afflicted, yet he did not open his mouth' (53:7). Jesus knew that his mission was about suffering and death. Yet, he chose to be obedient to the will of the Father. Again, Mark portrays Jesus as the suffering servant who suffers in silence.

A picture is starting to unfold of Mark's portrayal of Jesus as the suffering servant of Isaiah who suffered and died innocently because of the sin of the world. Mark establishes this picture mainly through allusions to Isaiah's Suffering Servant. Mark wants his readers to understand that Jesus' death served a purpose. However, it was not an egocentric purpose (cf. Thielman 2007:206-207). Neither did he die because of any sins he committed. Rather, Mark wants his readers to understand that Jesus suffered and died for many, including his disciples. Jesus died for both Jews and Gentiles who would believe in him as the Son of God. His death has a universal impact. He dies for people of all nations and times. Now that we have a preliminary picture of how Mark portrayed Jesus as Suffering Servant in his Gospel, it will be helpful to move to the second chapter where we will study Isaiah 40-55.

Chapter Two

The Two Faces of Suffering

In Mark 10:45b Jesus reveals why he had to come to earth. He lets his disciples know that he came to give his life as a ransom for many. Jesus uses words that echo the prophetic words of Isaiah 53:12. This raises the question of the picture which Isaiah presents of the suffering servant in the so-called servant songs.

Identification of Four Servant Songs

There are four servant songs which German scholar Bernhard Duhm identified as follows: First servant song 42:1-4, (9); second servant song 49:1-6, (13); third servant song 50:4-9, (11); and the fourth servant song 52:13-53:12 (cf. Adam 2006:104). These songs suggest that the servant is the Messiah. Duhm holds that the servant songs were written at a later stage by another author other than Isaiah of the eighth century (:104). Thus, he calls the author of the servant songs Deutero-Isaiah. However, there is not sufficient evidence from the texts to support Duhm's Deutero-Isaiah theory (cf. Bultema 1981:362-373). Therefore, in this paper I will take the position that the prophet Isaiah is the author of the entire book of Isaiah including the four servant songs (cf. Kaiser 2012:87-88).

Background of Isaiah 40-55

Some people call *Isaiah* the Mount Everest of the Old Testament. It is among the most frequently quoted Old Testament books in the New Testament. The book is named after the prophet Isaiah, the son of Amoz, who was married to a prophetess and was the father of at least two sons (Isa 7:3; 8:3). His name, Isaiah, means 'The Lord is salvation'. Isaiah has been described as the 'Paul of the Old Testament' (e.g., Motyer 1999b:18).

The prophet Isaiah mainly directed his prophecies to Judah and Israel during the years 739-681 B.C. He prophesied during the reigns of Uzziah, Jotham, Ahaz and

Hezekiah (Isaiah 1:1), who were the kings of Judah between 715 and 686 B.C. It was during these years that Israel struggled politically and spiritually. Their condition did not improve, but rather weakened in such a way that the Northern Kingdom of Israel fell into the hands of the Assyrian Empire in 722 B.C. The Southern Kingdom, Judah, was facing a similar fate. Like Israel, they were socially and religiously corrupt. It was during this time of political and spiritual struggle that the prophet Isaiah came to proclaim to Judah that they should trust God who had promised them a wonderful kingdom. Isaiah encouraged them not to seek assistance from Egypt or any other foreign nation that could protect them against Assyria. In all of this, the Lord was their only protector and the one who would deliver them out of the hardship (Martin 1985:1030).

Isaiah 39 gives us a clue to the events that occur in chapters 40-55. These events were already mentioned by the prophet Isaiah in chapter 9, verses 1-4. During the time of Assyria's attack, King Hezekiah, who was miraculously healed by God after a serious illness, sought to be friends with Assyria's enemies. Hezekiah displayed God's treasures to the Babylonians who were sent by the king of Babylon. Hezekiah's pride caused the people of Israel to be taken into captivity by Babylon (Wolf 1998:1047-1048). The treasures of God, which Hezekiah displayed, were also taken to Babylon (Isaiah 39:5-7).

By the time this prophecy regarding Israel's captivity was realised, the prophet Isaiah was no longer alive. Yet, his words could still speak comfort to those who would experience that difficult time in Israel's history. Israel had been unfaithful to God; they had not obeyed his laws. Instead, they had chosen to worship idols (Isaiah 42:8, 24). In other words, Israel was in captivity because of their sin and God's wrath against their sin. Not only did the prophet Isaiah predict the punishment, but he also foretold that God would release Israel from bondage in Babylon (Wolf 1998:1047-1048). However, there was more to Israel's release. Although Israel deserved to be punished for their sins, God stretched out his arm to redeem them from their bondage of sin (Isaiah 43:1).

In Isaiah 40:2 God announced that Israel's 'hard service (translates the Hebrew word for "warfare") has been completed and that her sins have been paid for' (Young

1972:22). Hereby, God also proclaimed that he would redeem Israel. But how and through whom will God redeem Israel? In Isaiah 42:1, God introduces his Servant, 'Here is my servant, whom I uphold, my chosen one in whom I delight.' The Servant will act as the arm of God to redeem Israel, but his arm will also be stretched to redeem all other people besides Israel (Isaiah 40:11; 41:10; 53:1). The significance of the mission of the servant is that he is tasked to redeem all nations from sin, even the Gentiles.

The Role of the Servant in Isaiah 40-55

Initially, the nation of Israel was referred to as the servant of the Lord (Isaiah 41:8; 42:19; 43:10; 44:1-2, 21; 45:4; 48:20), but unexpectedly in Isaiah 42:1 another servant is introduced (Motyer 1999b:26). There is something different about this servant. Not only has God put his Spirit on this Servant (Isaiah 42:1), but the characteristics of this individual and the role assigned to him differ significantly from the nation of Israel (cf. Alexander 1998:108-109). The first and most remark-able difference is that the nation of Israel is blind and deaf (Isaiah 42:18-20; 43:8; 48:8, 18-20). This blindness and deafness caused Israel to be disobedient to God. 'But the Servant who only appears in chapters 40-48 and then three times in chapters 49-50, is always obedient and responsive to God' (Oswalt 1998:470). Even though the conditions under which the Servant carried out the task are harsh, he remained obedient (Isaiah 42:2-4). A second difference is that this Servant was introduced with a double task, whereas the task of Israel as servant was to display God's glory among the nations. However, that is exactly what Israel failed to do and why another servant is needed to fulfil God's will (cf. Goldingay 2014:66-68).

The Persian king Cyrus appears suddenly in Isaiah 45:1-4 as Israel's redeemer. He is described as the one who delivers Israel from Babylon (Isaiah 41:25). The Servant who is being introduced in Isaiah 42:1 would be more significant than Cyrus the Persian king. Cyrus will only deliver Israel from Babylon. The Servant is the one who delivers Israel and the world from sin (Wolf 1998:1051). Israel, as God's servant (chosen nation) was supposed to bring other nations to the knowledge of God but because of their sin they failed. Martin (1985:1031) claims that the prophet

Isaiah was aware of the Abrahamic and Mosaic Covenants which stipulated the conditions of the covenants. Because Israel failed to obey the covenant law (Gen. 12:2-3; Deut. 28: 1-14; 28:15-68), the individual servant had to come to fulfil the will of God.

First Servant Song: Isaiah 42:1-4 (5-9)

In the context of Isaiah 42 and Isaiah 49, Israel is also named the servant (42:19; 44: 21; 49: 3). God chose Israel to be the servant, but they failed. The individual servant in Isaiah 42:1-4 is chosen to be the Servant-Messiah; the one whom God anointed (42:1; 43; 10; 49:5-6) to bring justice to the nations (42:1b) (Martin 1985:1095). This individual servant is introduced without identification. This servant song 42:1-9 consists of two parts. In the first part, 42:1-4, the Lord speaks of the Servant's task, and in the second part, 42:5-9, the Lord directs again his words to the Servant. The Lord confirms the task that he has given to the Servant in 42:1- 4. The Individual servant was tasked to bring justice to Israel and the islands (Isaiah 42:1d-4c). We are compelled to ask what kind of justice the Servant must bring to the nation.

Motyer (1999a:318) explains that justice is the key idea of this first servant song and that justice has a three-fold meaning. According to Motyer, the first meaning of justice is displayed in court, where a trial between the Lord and the idols takes place (:319). The outcome of the trial is that the individual servant must take the message to the ends of the world proclaiming that there is only one God. Motyer further suggests that the second meaning of justice portrays the individual servant to bring God's truth to the world (:319). The third and final meaning of justice is 'the righting of wrongs, and the establishment of a just order' (:319). John Goldingay (1984) supports what Motyer writes about the third meaning of justice. He suggests that justice is the sorting out of rights and wrongs to make true life possible (:94). The Servant's primary task in this song was to bring justice to the ends of the world. Justice connotes the idea of bringing the truth to the light. Thus, in the context of 42:1-4, the suggestions of both Motyer and Goldingay are fitting. This brings us to the second servant song, Isaiah 49:1-13.

Second Servant Song: Isaiah 49:1-7, (8-9)

We have seen that God's plan is for the Servant to bring forth justice to the ends of the world. Through this act of God, the Servant will bring sinners into a new covenant relationship with himself through the forgiveness of sins. As a result, he will restore Israel and the world into a right-standing position with himself. The preceding chapters (40-48) dealt mainly with Cyrus and his liberation of Israel from captivity. The following chapters (49-55) primarily focus on the Servant-Messiah fulfilling the task assigned to him.

Isaiah 49:1 begins with the Servant as the one who is addressing the islands and distant nations. The Servant is calling them to listen to him because of his special calling in 49:1-5. There is some similarity between verses 1c, d and 5b. All these verses are about the Servant who speaks about his calling. The Servant stresses that even before he was born, he was called to fulfil the special mission of the Servant. Here in verse 3, the Servant is called Israel and in verse 5 we are told that the Servant is to draw Israel back to God (Isaiah 49:5). Why then is the Servant called Israel?

The individual servant is the one who fulfils what the nation Israel failed to accomplish. Israel was chosen to be God's holy nation among the other nations, but they failed to fulfil their mission (Wright 2005:162). As a result, the Servant became Israel to portray God's holiness to the other nations. According to Motyer (1991a:383), in this second servant song, it is revealed that the Servant has a double task that involves Israel and the world. Motyer explains that in 49:1c-3 the Servant is first prepared and then named Israel (:385). He further explains that in 49:5 the Servant has been prepared and then appointed to redeem Israel. In 49:6 the Servant's second task is made known, i.e., that he is also to redeem nations worldwide (:385). David Jackman (2010:211) notes that '[t]he hope which flows from the servant's work extends [...] to the whole world.' Martin (1985:1048) states that the Lord promised to strengthen the Servant for this special task. The Servant will be despised and hated by the nations (49:7; 53:3), but it is the Servant who will be a light to the Gentiles (49:6). It is by God's strength that the Servant will fulfil his double task to bring Israel back to God and to be a light to the Gentiles (49:6, 8-9). Martin claims that the Servant's success is already assured by the promise that kings and princes will see the Servant and bow down to him (49:7) (:1049).

The first Servant song portrays a picture of the Servant who is commissioned to bring justice to the end of the world. The second song reveals that the Servant had a double task to bring Israel back to God and the Servant had to be a light to the Gentiles.

Third Servant Song: Isaiah 50:4-9

Barry Webb (1996:198) suggests that the Servant is the one speaking in Isaiah 50:4-9: 'Once more the Servant speaks, letting us into some of the most deeply personal areas of his life: his communion with God, the physical and mental suffering which marks his way, and the assurance of final vindication that buoys him up.' Webb adds that the Servant 'speaks more to himself than to others' (:198). In contrast to Isaiah 49:2, the Servant's mouth was a sharp sword. In this third song, the Servant is now a student-teacher who obediently listens to the instructions of the Lord. The Servant is not rebellious against the instruction of the Lord. Martin (1985:1104-1105) notes that the Servant obediently endures the suffering that his special task involves. He is obedient to the end (50:5; 53: 6- 7).

Israel is punished because of their rebellion, while it is the Servant's obedience that causes him to be punished and beaten (50:6; 53: 3-5). Amid so much violent opposition the Servant expresses strong confidence. The Servant knows his mission will be about rejection and suffering (50:6). Yet, he is the one to offer comfort to his followers, while he holds on to his final vindication (Isaiah 50:4-9, 11). Motyer (1999a:398) and Martin (1985:1104-1105) both suggest that this song portrays more of the suffering and obedience of the Servant. Jackman (2010:216) adds:

> We are not told at whose hands he suffers, or what task he is trying to perform. It is clear that his obedience to the word of the sovereign Lord has brought about the confrontation, but he faces this with great confidence in God's protection and vindication.

Isaiah 42:1-4 presents the Servant as one with the mission 'to bring justice to the nations'. In 49:1-7 the Servant is again presented, but this time with a double task relating to Israel and the world. In 50:4-9 the Servant himself speaks, sharing about the suffering he is to face. Yet no reason is given for this suffering (Young 1972:335). Might it be that the reason why the Servant had to undergo so much suffering will be found in the fourth and final servant song?

The Fourth Servant Song: Isaiah 52:13-53:12

Young (1972:355) suggests that Isaiah 52:13-15 is an introduction to Isaiah 53:1-12 and that these verses concern the Servant of the Lord. Goldingay (1984:141) argues that the picture that has been portrayed of the Servant is that of one who was considered a nobody. The Servant suffers in so many ways of rejection and sorrow even to the point of death. The suffering of the Servant portrays a distorted image of the true image of the Servant, who is the Messiah. The Servant had no beauty, no majesty, he was regarded as hopeless and worthless (53:1-3). Goldingay suggests that there was nothing impressive or handsome about the Servant that would draw your attention to him (52:14) (:141). He suffered and was rejected because he took the iniquities of 'others' on himself. The people thought it was because of the Servant's sin that he was afflicted by God (Martin 1985:1106-1107). However, the Servant suffered and bore the wrath of God for the sins of 'others' (53: 3-6; 50:6). The Servant was unfairly tried and cut off from the land of the living (53:8). One can say that his fate was undeserved. Being cut off left the Servant without dignity, hope and life. Philip Hacking (2001:149) comments: 'There is nothing neatly theological here. Rather we are faced with deep human suffering.'

The first (Isaiah 42:1) and fourth (Isaiah 52:13) servant songs begin with the words 'Here is my Servant' and 'See, my Servant'. Motyer (1999a:424) suggests that this gives the impression that the Lord wanted the focus to be constantly on the Servant. Also, that a major change is about to happen in the world because of the Servant, or at least in the history of Israel/Judah. Disappointment must have filled many about the Servant, because of his un-majestic appearance, suffering, rejection and death. However, he would be vindicated and exalted above all. But why was it necessary for him to suffer so much?

The Purpose of the Servant's Suffering

Wright (2005:161) believes that the nation Israel failed in their mission as 'God's servant to bring glory to him among the nations as his witness'. Israel's failure not only disqualified them as the servant of God, but their sins brought them under God's judgement. Wright affirms that 'Israel was blind, deaf and incapacitated. They need to be brought back to God, not just back to Jerusalem' (:161). God raised Cyrus, the king of Persia, to liberate Israel from Babylonian captivity and bring his people back to Jerusalem (Isaiah 45:1-4). Wright asks the question, 'who then will restore Israel spiritually?' (:161).

We recall that the second servant song Isaiah 49:1-7 presented the Servant with a double task relating to Israel and the world. The Servant had a mission to Israel, to restore them to God and be a light to the Gentiles (49:6). The execution of this mission caused the Servant suffering and death (53:10). The Servant alone was righteous; therefore, he had been made a guilt offering for the sin of Israel and the world.

The term 'Guilt offering' points us to Leviticus 5-7 (Ellen 2012:178-179). In its context, the offering served as an atoning sacrifice for sin. In Isaiah 40-55 the Servant fulfils his task by becoming the guilt offering for Israel and the world's sin. He becomes the Suffering Servant who poured out his life for many. We now understand why the Servant needed to suffer and die. He was made the guilt offering for everybody's sin. This prompts the question, 'Does Mark in his portrayal of Jesus also see Jesus as the one who poured out his life as a guilt offering for all?'

The aspect on which Mark focuses might not be as obvious as it is in Isaiah, but when we look at the way Mark develops his gospel, we see that the suffering servant/messiah image stands out. Just as Isaiah proclaims that the good news begins with a messenger and culminates with the coming of 'the Lord', Mark similarly introduces his Gospel as the beginning of the good news about Jesus Christ, the Son of God (Mark 1:1). The uncertainty that surrounds the identification of the suffering servant in Isaiah, however, is also present in Mark's Gospel. This can be seen in the question 'Who is this man, Jesus?' which the Jewish authorities, crowds and the disciples raised ever since Jesus began his public ministry (Mark 1:27, 34, 44; 3:12; 5:43; 7:36; 8:26, 30) (4:41; 6:1-3, 51; 7:37; 8:21).

The Son of God Became a Servant

The climax is reached with Peter's confession 'You are the Christ' (Mark 8:29). This revelation was indeed the good news that Mark wanted to bring across to the readers about Jesus, the Son of God (Mark 1:1, 11). We should have thought that such good news needed to be proclaimed from the rooftops as the Jewish people were waiting for the Messiah to come. However, in Mark 8:30 we read that the Messiah himself warned the disciples not to tell others that he was the Messiah. Why would Jesus silence the disciples? The answer is that the people expected a kingly type of Messiah, a political figure who would set them free from Roman rule (Garland 1996:323-324).

Considering Jesus' warning not to tell anybody that he is the Christ, we are prompted to ask: 'What does it then mean to be 'the Christ'? Although Mark indicates in the opening of his Gospel that Jesus is the Christ, it is not until Peter's confession that Jesus speaks plainly about his purpose and mission as the Christ (8:31-32). It seems as if Peter's confession creates the opportunity for Jesus to reveal the purpose of his mission as the Christ. Edwards (2002:252) affirms that only after Peter has called Jesus Messiah, Jesus begins to teach the disciples what it means to be the Christ. Jesus' teaching had a *negative* undertone that implies that the Messiah would become the servant of all through his suffering and death.

The Son of Man Must Suffer and Sacrifice Himself

It was either a 'surprise' or a 'shock' to the disciples that Jesus' messiahship involved suffering and death. Peter's reaction to the announcement of the first passion prediction shows that they did not understand at all (Mark 8:32-33), that the Son of Man *must* suffer and die. According to their expectation, the Messiah would reign as king over the whole world (cf. Garland 1996:323-327) or as William Placher (2010:116) explains:

31

> For all the differences in the pictures of the Messiah anticipated by various first-century Jews, they shared a hope of triumph. Somehow the Messiah would win victories, defeat Israel's enemies, restore Israel's greatness. The idea of a suffering Messiah was radically new.

A king who is going to die was beyond comprehension and simply not acceptable. To sum it up, in Edwards' words 'the meaning of Jesus' life and mission is not about victory and success, but about rejection, suffering and death. When Jesus finally speaks to the issue of his identity and mission it is summed up in 'The Son of Man must suffer many things' (2002:253).

The suffering of Jesus reached its climax at the cross when the centurion stood in front of Jesus. The centurion heard Jesus' cry and saw him die. As a result, he declared 'Surely, this man was the Son of God' (Mark 15:39). It took so much suffering, rejection and Jesus' death for people to realize that Mark's Jesus was indeed the true Messiah, i.e., the one whom God has chosen and anointed as his only beloved Son. At the cross humanity truly recognized Jesus as the Son of God. Being the Christ, the Son of God is what caused Jesus so much suffering and ultimately death. This is the main aspect that Mark wants his readers to grasp. The purpose and mission of Jesus, the Christ (Mark10:45) was fulfilled at the cross (Mark 15:39). At the cross the Messiah sacrificed himself for many.

Chapter Three

Christological Images

Since Jesus' appearance on the scene, questions were asked about him. The demonic spirits were the first to ask, 'What do you want with us? Have you come to destroy us?' (Mark 1:24). While the crowds who were amazed by his teachings ask, 'What is this? A new teaching, a new authority?' (1:27), the religious leaders who took offence at Jesus expressed their disagreement by asking questions like 'Why does this fellow talk like this? Who can forgive sins but God alone?' (2:7), 'Why does he eat with sinners?' (2:16), 'Why does he not keep the rules on the Sabbath?' (2:24), 'Where did he get all this from?' (6:2), or 'Isn't this just the carpenter's son?' (6:3). The question the disciples raised after the calming of the storm, 'Who is this man?' (4:41) points us to the real issue: Who is Jesus? (Wright 2005:103-104).

Son of God

Mark's use of the title *Son of God* in the opening verse of his gospel indicates the importance that this title holds (cf. Cranfield 1979:37-38). As the narrative develops there are times that Mark lifts the veil when he introduces his readers to key events, such as Jesus' baptism (Mark 1:11) and the transfiguration (9:7), where God affirms Jesus' sonship. The same is true for Jesus' encounters with demons, and their recognition of who Jesus is, i.e., the Holy One of God (Mark 1:24; 3:11; 5:7). The meaning of divine sonship becomes obvious at Jesus' baptism. The declaration of the voice from heaven, 'You are my son' (1:11) is the first identification of Jesus as the Son of God. Bauer (1992:772-773) suggests that *Son of God* is an important and central title in Mark's Gospel. Thus, it occurs eight times in the Gospel (1:1, 11; 3:11; 5:7; 9:7; 13:32; 14:61; 15:39). Each time we can find it in a crucial episode. Peter Lewis (2004:183) concludes: 'Mark leaves his readers in no doubt about the supernatural character of Jesus' sonship. It cannot be 'reduced' to an honorific title as in some Old Testament texts.'

The climax is reached with the Roman centurion's confession at the cross (Mark 15:39). Throughout his public ministry, Jesus was reluctant to use the phrase 'Son of God'. The reason behind the secrecy is that Jesus did not want to be proclaimed as such, because Jesus' sonship involved suffering and death (Bauer 1992:772-773). But now there is no need for such secrecy anymore and so the centurion proclaims 'Surely, this man was the Son of God!'. Sinclair Ferguson (2002:264) comments:

> Exactly, what the centurion meant by his words we do not really know. But Mark at least invites his readers to make his words their own. Throughout the Gospel, [...], he brings us back time and again to face the question: Who is Jesus? Here, in his weakness and rejection, Jesus is seen to be none other than the Son of God.

Son of Man

Although Jesus knew that he is the Son of God, he preferred to use the title 'the Son of Man' (Mark 8:31). The words 'Son of Man' occurs fourteen times in Mark's Gospel (2:10, 28; 8:31, 38; 9:9, 12, 31; 10:33, 45; 13:26; 14:21a, b, 41, 62b). The title was only used by Jesus. In Edward's (2002:79) opinion 'it was a rather ambiguous title largely free of the political connotations associated with Messiah.' The phrase seemed unimportant to his hearers, and many times Jesus used it in the face of opposition and hostility. He used it in such a way that his hearers might discover his identity. Yet, despite Jesus' intentions the Jewish leaders failed many times to grasp his true identity (:80).

As in the other two synoptic gospels, references to the Son of Man in Mark's Gospel can be divided into three categories. There are those Son of Man sayings that refer to Jesus' authority over sickness, sin and nature (2:10, 28). Others portend Jesus' coming suffering, rejection, death and resurrection (8:31; 9:31; 10:33). Finally, there are those that refer to the eschatological coming of the Son of Man in glory (8:38; 13:26; 14:62) (Wright 2005:150-151). Edwards (2002:80) suggests 'that each category refers to a divine attribute.' He further argues that the second category of references that speak of his suffering is fulfilling a divinely ordained purpose

(:80). Edwards describes Jesus' authority to forgive sins (2:10) as an allusion to the Son of Man figure in Daniel 7:13-14 (:80). Similarly, Blomberg (1997:406) notes:

> Seeing a Danielic background for the title allows one to accept sayings in all three categories as authentic. The vision of a heavenly man clearly fits the exalted sayings […]. The references to oppression and war against the saints in Daniel 7:21, 25 could have suggested the link with suffering […] Even in the sayings that seem least dependent on a Danielic background hints of either suffering or exaltation seem present.

Messiah and Son of David

The Hebrew title *Messiah* (*masiah*), which means *the anointed one*, occurs 39 times in the Old Testament, while its Greek equivalent *Christ* (*Christos*) can be found 529 times in the New Testament (Farmer 1994: 570-571). Mark introduces his Gospel as the gospel about the Messiah (Christ). Christ is commonly used in contemporary Christian language as a kind of surname, and few Christians, it seems, understand the deeper meaning of the phrase and its significance in the New Testament.

In the Old Testament, the word *anointed* is not used for a future messianic figure who would come to save Israel (Kelhoffer & McRay 1996:408). However, what we find in the Old Testament are many examples of kings, priests and prophets who were anointed for special tasks at different times (e.g. Isaiah 61:1, 1 Samuel 12:3, Leviticus 4:5). Such anointing carries the idea of being set aside by God for God's purposes. The title Messiah appears in most English translations only in Daniel 9:25-26. Wright (2005:143) explains that the prophecy of Daniel is about 'an anointed one who will come and bring to a climax God's purpose, which is summed up in the words, 'to finish transgression, to put an end to sin, to atone for wickedness.'

Wright (1992:143) draws our attention to Isaiah 45:1 which indicates that God himself anointed Cyrus, the pagan king of Persia as his agent. This was an unusual act, because, as Wright notes, 'Cyrus was not an Israelite, certainly not a king in the line of David' (:144). However, by describing Cyrus as 'his messiah' we learn much about the meaning of that phrase at the time (:144). Thus, Cyrus' anointing serves several purposes (:144). Firstly, God chose and raised Cyrus for a specific assign-ment (41:2ff, 25). Secondly, he achieved what God wanted him to achieve. In other words, God worked through him as his agent (44:28; 45:15). Thirdly, God ordained Cyrus to redeem and restore Israel from the hands of their adversaries (44:28; 45:13). Fourthly, God would use all of Cyrus' military achievements and his authority for liberating the people of God. Fifthly and finally, Cyrus as the anointed one of God would be used by God to take his salvation beyond Israel to the ends of the earth. Wright notes:

> All of these were features in the developing messianic concept in post-Old Testament times, particularly as associated with the expectation of a coming son of David. The Messiah would be God's agent to deliver and restore Israel, not a pagan king this time, but a true Israelite, the true son of David.

Similarly, Bauer (1992:766) explains that whenever the phrase *Son of David* is used as a Christological title it points to Jesus as the royal Messiah, while Jack Kingsbury (1989:55) writes that the designations *Son of David*, *Son of God* and *King of the Jews* are all messianic titles. In other words, Mark portrays Jesus as the Davidic Messiah-King who ultimately fulfils God's promise made to David:

> I will raise up your offspring to succeed you, your own flesh and blood, and I will establish his kingdom. He is the one who will build a house for my Name, and I will establish the throne of his kingdom for ever. I will be his father, and he shall be my son […] (2 Samuel. 7:12-16).

In 12:35-37, Mark tells us how Jesus raised the issue regarding the Messiah's identity. Jesus asked his audience in the temple courts, 'Why do the teachers of the law say that the Messiah is the son of David?' Jesus does not reject the identification of the Messiah as the son of David. On the contrary, he acknowledges this identifi-cation. However, his question implies, as Hurtado (1998:203) notes, that the com-mon understanding of the Messiah as the Davidic son is inadequate. He continues to explain:

The work of the Messiah is to be far greater than that of David. It involves redemption for all peoples and not just for Israel. In other words, the question about the Messiah's relationship to David is not about his family line [..] the passage suggests that the full significance of Jesus as Messiah cannot be measured by connecting him with David. The divinely inspired David is quoted as connecting the Messiah with the throne of God [...], suggesting that the true Messiah is to be understood as bearing not only Davidic, but also divine significance (:204).

Harrington (2013:96) concludes that while *Son of David* is a traditional Jewish title it is not an adequate title, because it does not really describe the character of Jesus' messiahship.

Christological Titles and the Suffering Servant

Mark uses various Christological titles and designations to communicate Jesus' significance (Le Roux 2018:154). But how are these titles and designations related to the image of the Suffering Servant?

The Son of God and the Suffering Servant

Lewis (2004:183) notes that Jesus' sonship is 'essential to Mark's portrayal and goes to the heart of his Christology.' The phrase sonship has a variety of meanings, such as knowledge, intimate fellowship, obedience or special work (Bauer 1992:770). All these aspects apply to Jesus. Two aspects, however, are of particular importance. The first one is the personal and intimate relationship that Jesus enjoyed with his heavenly Father. He often spoke to God in prayer and addressed him as Abba (Mark 14:36), an Aramaic term meaning father. According to Bauer (1992:772), 'Abba was a term of familiarity and intimacy that originally developed from the speech of children.' Another indication of the closeness between Jesus and the Father is the declaration made by the latter at Jesus' baptism: 'You are my Son, whom I love; with you I am well pleased.' (Mark 1:11). Walter Wessel (1984:622) comments: 'The main emphasis, however, is on the unique sonship of Jesus. Mark confesses Jesus as Son of God at the very outset of his Gospel (1:1). Here God confesses Jesus as his Son.'

The second aspect is the Son's obedience to the will of the Father. The Father's words 'With you I am well pleased', spoken at the Son's baptism, demonstrate that God has absolute confidence in Jesus (cf. Wessel 1994:622). He is the obedient son who will fulfil his mission. This divine declaration alludes to both Isaiah 42:1, 'Here is my servant, whom I uphold, my chosen one in whom I delight', and Isaiah 49:3 'You are my servant, Israel, in whom I will display my splendour.' It thus links the concept of sonship with that of the servant of Yahweh. Bauer (1992:772) notes that divine sonship is defined in its relation to obedience, and obedience is related to the image of the servant.

Edwards (2002:15) points out that 'Jesus lived in a time where various heroes or divine men of the Hellenistic world were ranked above the characteristics of the world. In this atmosphere, in a distressed world, Jesus had to model his divine sonship.' Therefore, he supports the idea that the son's obedience to the will of the Father was wrapped up in suffering and death. Edwards writes that the 'key to understanding the Son of God is in his suffering. The Son of God had to be obedient to the will of the Father even if it involved death (Mark 14:36)' (:15).

That Jesus fully understood his identity and mission as the Son of God and the role that suffering played in that mission can be seen in the words he prayed in the garden of Gethsemane, 'Abba Father [...] everything is possible for you. Take this cup from me. Yet not what I will, but what you will' (14:36). Jesus' request that he might be spared the shameful and painful death at a Roman cross is immediately followed by his acceptance of what he knows is central to God's salvation plan for humankind. Hurtado (1998:242) speaks of a powerful example of submission to God's will, which Mark's readers were to emulate in times of hardship. He continues: 'Mark's account is not motivated by a desire to give a sentimental picture of Jesus, but it is intended to give his readers a role model to follow. It reflects a practical concern for their ability to stand firm in trials of their faith' (:242).

The Son of Man and the Suffering Servant

In Mark 10:45, Jesus reveals that 'the Son of Man' has come to serve others and to give his life as a ransom for many. This is an important verse that links the Son of

Man's mission with the mission of Isaiah's Suffering Servant (Isaiah 52:13-53:12). Garland (1996:413) points out that the word 'ransom' was used for a variety of payments, such as the compensation for a crime or personal injury or the money given to free an enslaved family member. He continues, 'The concept of ransom [...] is connected to the idea of cost, substitution, and atonement. Isaiah 53:10-12 forms the most likely backdrop here' (:413).

Likewise, Wright (2005:154) notes 'that Jesus repeatedly linked this self-designation of Son of Man with his suffering, rejection and death.' He suggests that 'Jesus drew on another figure from his Hebrew bible, and that figure was the Servant of the Lord' (:154). In other words, Jesus' predictions of his suffering and death in Mark 8:31, 9:33 and 10:33, 45 relate to Isaiah's image of the suffering servant. In these predictions, Jesus combines his suffering and death with the future coming of the Son of Man, who will be vindicated and given authority (see Isaiah 52:13, 53:12 and Daniel 7:13-14). Marshall affirms that the language of Mark 9:12 and 10:45 suggests that the Son of Man experienced the sufferings of the suffering servant in Isaiah 52:13-53:12 (Marshall 1992:776). The self-designation *Son of Man* was the title Jesus used to reveal his mission. Vindication and exaltation await the Son of Man, but first, he must suffer and die, not for his own sin but for the sins of the whole world.

Furthermore, the suffering and rejection of the Son of Man resemble the suffering of God's holy people described in Daniel chapter 7. Thus, Daniel speaks of a fourth kingdom that 'will devour the whole earth, trampling it down and crushing it' (7:23) After that another king will come to power. 'He will speak against the Most High and oppress his holy people and try to change the set times and the laws. The holy people will be delivered into his hands for a time [...]' (:25). Daniel's language here is strikingly similar to the words of Jesus recorded by Mark in 10:33 where Jesus declares to his disciples: 'We are going up to Jerusalem [...] and the Son of Man will be delivered over to the chief priests and the teachers of the law.' Daniel's 'one like a Son of Man' can be seen as a representative of the saints of the Most High who suffer severely at the hands of their enemies. John Goldingay (1989:193) writes:

Talk of the holy ones being oppressed, however, could easily be transferred to the humanlike figure himself [...] and when Jesus goes on to speak of the Son of Man's calling to give his life as a ransom for many, the suffering of the holy one may have been one of the motifs in his mind [...] He is to be the one to whom every knee bows, but only after accepting the form of a servant and the humiliation of the cross (Phil 2:5-11).

The Messiah and the Suffering Servant

According to Wilfrid Harrington (2013:95), it is rather unlikely that Jesus ever claimed to be the Messiah. He continues to explain: 'It is very likely, on the other hand, that some of his followers thought him to be the Messiah. It is also very likely that Jesus' opponents may have understood him or his followers to claim that he was the Messiah' (:95). However, in Mark 9:41 we read how Jesus indirectly identifies as the Messiah by saying to his disciples 'Truly I tell you anyone who gives you a cup of water in my name because you belong to the Messiah will certainly not lose their reward.' Later, he is asked by the high priest 'Are you the Messiah, the Son of the Blessed One?' and Jesus responds in a straightforward way by saying: 'I am [...]' (14:61-62). However, during his earthly public ministry, he muted his claim to messiahship because those who believed in it misunderstood its nature (Wright 2005:148). Although the coming Messiah was not seen purely as a national hero or great military leader, 'his appearance was very much connected with the hope for a deliverance of the nation from the hands of oppressors and wicked men' (Hurtado 203:1998). Jesus, however, rejected the political and military notion attached to it. His understanding of his messianic role was a different one.

In 10:46-52 Mark tells us how Jesus shows practical compassion to a blind beggar called Bartimaeus who shouts 'Jesus, Son of David, have mercy on me!' when Jesus passes by. Jesus is on his way to Jerusalem, not to take part in a religious festival, but to die a painful death on a cross, and it is the first time that he is publicly addressed in such a way (Hewitt 1995:147). It seems that the blind Bartimaeus can see more than many of his fellow Israelites. What Bartimaeus has heard about Jesus convinces him that Jesus is the long-expected Messiah who can deliver him from his misery (:148), and Jesus does not disappoint him: "Go,' said Jesus, 'your faith has healed you." (10:52). Placher (2010:155) notes that Bartimaeus 'is someone who gets everything right.' He explains: 'He recognizes Jesus as the Messiah, gives up everything, asks only for his sight, and follows Jesus on the way. And who is this perfect disciple? A blind beggar, sitting by the roadside, yelling his head off for Jesus' (:155).

Jesus' compassionate response stands in stark contrast to the popular notion of the Messiah as a forceful political and military liberator. Jesus' response is rather a demonstration of the Messiah's mercy towards those in need, or as Ferguson (2002:177) puts it:

> His willingness to stop, when his own heart must have been heavy with sorrow; his concern that Bartimaeus should share his need, when not even his own disciples seemed capable of sharing their own need – all this emphasises the gracious character of the Saviour. It stands also in marked contrast to the events of the previous section, when the disciples had fought among themselves for the places of honour and Jesus reminded them that true greatness lies in humble service. If that is so, the Jesus' greatness never stood out more clearly than when he called this helpless man out of darkness and into the light of a new and more glorious way.

As the *Son of David* Jesus shows his messianic authority in works of compassion and healing for the marginalised like Bartimaeus (Garland 1996:420). In a short time, he will be executed as the messianic 'King of the Jews' (Mark 15:26). The notice nailed above his head states his crime. It is pure irony that Jesus is killed as a political messiah (Garland 1996:589). Lane (2010:568) explains the deeper meaning of the words written on a board and nailed to the cross on which the tortured body of Jesus hung:

> It is declared that Jesus had been sentenced to death as politically subver-sive of the authority of imperial Rome. The wording was designed to convey a subtle insult to Jewish pretensions and to mock all attempts to assert the sovereignty of a subject territory. The detail concerning the inscription, which conforms to Roman penal procedure and must reflect

eyewitness report, is a solid historical fact. It provides the impeachable information that Jesus went to his death as the Messiah.

Jesus died as the rejected kingly Messiah. Two rebels accompanied him in death (Mark 15:27). His death between these rebels, as Cole (2006:1199) notes, fulfils the prophecy of Isaiah 53:12.

Chapter Four

Christian Discipleship

Jesus' Suffering as a Model for Discipleship

Now that we have established that Mark portrays Jesus as the Suffering Servant of Isaiah 40-55, we need to ask the question, 'How can Jesus' suffering-humiliation, sacrifice and service be a model for his disciples?' To find an answer to this question we will examine those passages which deal with Jesus' teachings on servanthood. These passages come as a cluster in which Mark 10:45 (and the preceding verses) is of central importance.

Location	Passion Prediction	Blindness	Teaching	Paradox
Caesarea-Philippi	8:31	8:32	8:34-37	Save life/Lose life
Galilee to Judea	9:31	9:33	9:35-31	First/Last
On the way to Jerusalem	10:32-34	10:35-39	10:42-45	Greatest/least Servant

The cluster of teachings is framed by two healing stories (Mark 8:22-26; 10:46-52). It all unfolds along a journey to Jerusalem (10:32). Each teaching is preceded by a passion prediction (8:31; 9:31; 10:32-34). Immediately after each prediction the blindness of the disciples surfaces (8:32; 9:33; 10:35-39), and then follow the enigmatic teachings (see Myers 2002:8). We are going to exegete each teaching concerning Jesus' prediction that 'the Son of Man must suffer many things and die.' It was only after Peter's confession that Jesus is the Christ that Jesus openly spoke about his impending suffering and death (8:29, 31, 32). The disciples would not have understood the purpose behind Jesus' teaching if he had taught them before Peter's confession. Now, that the disciples knew that Jesus was the Christ, it would help them to understand what his talk about his impending suffering and death was all about.

The Blindness of the Disciples: Mark 8:32-33

The disciples' blindness was already an issue at the feeding of the four thousand and the Pharisees' attempt to test Jesus (8:17-18). Dickson Kagema (2014) notes that '[t]he disciples were blind to the true significance of Jesus and what he was doing. They did not understand Jesus' mission, as well as their own mission.' Their blindness would become more apparent as it would hinder them from grasping the true nature of discipleship. The fact that Peter rebuked Jesus shows that Jesus' revelation came as a surprise to him. Peter was not prepared for a Messiah who was going to suffer and die. Lane (2010:304) suggests that the rest of the disciples supported Peter's rebuke and views regarding the Messiah. Jesus responds by using strong language, 'Get behind me, Satan.' According to Lane, such a response was necessary because Jesus was aware that it might be part of Satan's plan to thwart the divine plan of salvation (:304). Jesus was determined to remain obedient to the will of the Father.

Requirements to Follow Christ: Mark 8:34-37

To follow Jesus required from the disciples personal commitment in situations that might involve danger and sacrifice. Lane (2010:305-306) argues that Mark added this section as an essential requirement for being a follower of Christ. He further suggests that in this section Mark is also expressing his pastoral concern for his readers. Jesus emphasized that suffering was not only his destiny but would also be the destiny of his disciples. It is noteworthy that Jesus included the crowd in this teaching. Lane explains that the calling of the crowd signified that being a follower of Jesus implies suffering to all believers and not just the disciples (:306).

Self-denial means that everyone who wants to follow Jesus must be willing to lose or give up everything for Jesus' sake. It does not mean the temporary loss of some luxury, but a totally new outlook on life, readjustment of values and priorities

(Grogan 1995:121). Likewise, taking up one's cross requires the active participation of everyone who confesses that Jesus is the Christ. Larry Hurtado's (1998:142) explanation of the phrase is particularly helpful: 'Take up his cross refers to the practice of making the condemned person carry the crossbeam upon which he was to be tied or nailed at the place of his execution.' It was a cruel, painful and humiliating exercise. Crucifixion, Geoffrey Grogan (1995:121) points out 'meant social ostracism and utter loneliness at a time of the deepest suffering.' In other words, by asking them to take up their cross Jesus is telling his disciples that they must be prepared to suffer physically and emotionally for his sake.

Considering this, Lane (2010:306) suggests that Jesus intended his disciples to be more than observers of his suffering. Jesus wanted his disciples and all believers to grow in faith and understanding through participation in his suffering. That is why the calling for denial and taking up of one's cross is not optional but a requirement. Because it is only through one's own experience of suffering that one can begin to understand Jesus' suffering. Physical suffering and humiliation were a reality for Jesus, and they would become a reality not only for his disciples but also for Mark's readers.

Life on earth is regarded as the most precious gift. Therefore, human beings will do anything not to lose it. Yet, all their attempts not to lose their lives, are ultimately just as paradoxical as Jesus' statement in Mark 8:35, 'For whoever wants to save his life will lose it, but whoever loses his life for me will save it.' This verse seems complicated and can easily be misunderstood. It needs to be read in context to make sense. Thus, Cole (2006:1185) writes: 'Saving one's life (or refusal to die to self) inevitably results in spiritual death; losing one's life (self-denial or surrender of life and will to God) for the cause of Christ and the gospel inevitably leads to spiritual life.' Similarly, Edwards (2002:257) explains that 'to lose one's life is to lose physical existence on earth, but to lose one's soul has eternal worth'. The soul cannot be saved by preserving it, but by losing it to Christ. But what does it mean to lose one's soul to Christ? Edwards puts it in simple words: whoever clings here on earth to his own self and does not want to renounce all his existence to Jesus by following him completely will lose the opportunity of gaining eternal life. But the one for whom the earthly life has lost its value and who surrenders his all to Christ will have eternal life (Lane 2010:308). To be a follower of Christ requires disowning oneself, taking up of the cross and losing one's life. Put differently, followers of Christ need to be willing to make sacrifices. Jesus sacrificed himself for his disciples and everybody who will confess that Jesus is the Messiah. His sacrifice is exemplary for every believer who wants to be a follower of Christ. However, we should bear in mind that there is a difference between Jesus' atoning death and our suffering or death which are only for the sake of Christ but not atoning in nature.

Vital Teachings in the Areas of Humility and Suffering: Mark 9:30-45

The statement of Mark 8:35 'whoever wants to be a follower of Christ must lose his life' must have still been echoing in the ears and hearts of the disciples when Jesus again, for the second time, declared that the suffering, rejection and death of the Son of Man was inevitable. According to Edwards (2002:282), this passion prediction announces not only the suffering, rejection and death that awaited Jesus, but it also serves as a model of the life to which Jesus called the disciples. This understanding of discipleship was vastly different from the popular view, which saw it as a lifestyle of prestige and authority. In this passage, there is a location change. The previous site was Caesarea-Philippi. Now Jesus and the disciples were passing through Galilee and *on the way*, Jesus taught the disciples about the second prediction. Jesus did not want others to know about their whereabouts and that this teaching was meant primarily for the disciples (9:30-31).

Jesus' statement as Mark records it in chapter 9, verse 31, 'The Son of Man is going to be betrayed into the hands of men. They will kill him, and after three days he will rise.', is the most general one of the three passion predictions. Lane claims that this formulation lacks the undertone of divine commission. It rather communicates that Jesus' suffering and death are certain. They are so certain that Jesus' divine task can be described as already accomplished (Lane 2010:336-337). In his study Edwards (2002:283) illustrates Jesus' humanity by stressing that 'he who lives as a man among men will suffer under them.' Jesus, as the one who gives his life for others, will die at the hands of human beings. The first prediction showed that the priests, teachers of the law and elders were responsible for Jesus' suffering. Here, Edwards indicates that the second prediction is proof that Jesus will suffer at the hands of humanity (:283).

Lane (2010:337) notes that the betrayal or hand-over of the Son of Man is a new element. The fact that the Son of Man is handed over implies the fulfilment of God's will as expressed in Scripture. Edwards (2002:284) argues that the hand-over is part of the fulfilment of Christ's divine commission to die for the benefit of others, including those at whose hands he is to die. Put differently, Jesus is handed over by the Jewish leaders and all humankind (8:31; 9:31). The process of hand-over is a process of humiliation and suffering. Jesus, the Son of God, will be humiliated and suffer at the hands of human beings. According to Edwards, this is what Jesus aimed to teach his disciples, i.e. that the Son of Man must suffer and die. Yet, they did not understand what he meant. The debate among the disciples along the way testifies to their inability to grasp the teachings of Jesus.

In 9:33-36, Mark tells how Jesus confronts his disciples about a debate which they had along the way by asking them, 'What were you arguing about on the road?' (9:33). The disciples, however, keep silent. Their silence resembles that of the Pharisees in Mark 3:4. The reason for their silence is the same: both parties are guilty of shame and hardness of heart (Edwards 2002:285-286). The disciples know that what they were discussing on the road was inappropriate for the followers of a man who was willing to lay down his life for them (Hewitt 1995:129). Edwards and Lane suggest that the disciples' desire for recognition can be explained with their cultural context in which power and rank played an important role. Hurtado (1998) is more specific by pointing to common practice within religious groups and communities at that time. He explains:

> Some might think it strange for grown men to be arguing about who was the greatest among them [...]. But in the context of such groups as the religious sect at Qumran [...], where the whole community was ranked annually according to the worthiness of each individual, it does not appear strange for members of Jesus' band to have thought along similar lines (:153).

Jesus's words, 'If anyone wants to be first, he must be the very last, and the servant of all' (Mark 9:35) did not match with the disciples' desire for greatness. They wanted to be recognized for their association with Jesus. Peter's statement 'we have left everything to follow you' (10:28) exposes what they were hoping for. They wanted to be the sole beneficiaries of Jesus' power and glory. How different is their desire for recognition from Jesus' willingness to accept humiliation and suffering? Harrington (2013:136) helpfully comments: 'Jesus acknowledges that there is greatness in discipleship, greatness of service. And this is so because the loving service of the least member of the community is service of Jesus and of the Father.'

Edwards (2002:287) affirms that 'the model of service and humiliation that Jesus taught could only be heard on the road of humiliation to Jerusalem.' Jesus' closing remark in 9:50 'and be at peace with each' other stresses the importance of service and love above rank and recognition. Discipleship includes service to others, sacrifice and humiliation, as seen in the life of the Messiah. Jesus' statement in Mark 10:45 'For even the Son of Man did not come to be served, but to serve, and to give his life as a ransom for many' is like a seal of the true meaning of discipleship. This verse can be seen as the conclusion of a cluster of teachings concerning discipleship.

Understanding the Way of the Cross: Mark: 10:32-45

Leaders are people who influence other people. They are people who have been given authority. Authority is what James and John had in mind when they approached Jesus and asked him to be seated at his left and right side in his kingdom. They desired rank and prestige. 'The place of greatest honour', Hewitt (1995:145) notes, 'was the seat to the right of the king, and the seat on the left was the next most important.' Edwards points out that the request of James and John was in stark contrast to Jesus' humility and self-sacrifice. Similarly, Lane argues that the request of the sons of Zebedee shows that despite Jesus' efforts to impart in them a spirit of self-denial, they still misinterpreted what Jesus meant when he spoke about discipleship. Their ambition for power and honour revealed their ignorance of the true natures of both discipleship and God's kingdom. 'By contrast, the other ten disciples might have come out of this incident well', as Donald English (1996:182) notes, 'but when they learned what had happened they showed their anger with James and John, perhaps at being upstaged by them!' In other words, James and John failed, but so did the other ten disciples. Their indignant response reveals that they were driven by an ambition for greatness, too.

How many times do we fail because of our desire for power? The effect of such desire is often blindness. Power-driven people become blind to the truth of God's will. It prevents them from seeing the needs of others and opportunities to serve those in need. James and John's request unmasks their blindness. They had totally misunderstood Jesus and his teachings by seeking places of power and prestige. They could not see that Jesus was hugely different from any earthly king, and so was his kingdom. They even failed to see that they were motivated by pure selfishness. Edwards (2002:322) comments: 'How easily worship and discipleship are blended with self-interest; or worse, self-interest is masked as worship and discipleship.' The two sons of Zebedee and the rest of the disciples had to learn that discipleship comes with a price.

When James and John, the sons of Zebedee, came to Jesus and stood there in front of him, the difference between them and the Son of God could not be more obvious: Jesus had come to give and to serve; and what they wanted was to receive and rule. 'Teacher, we want you to do for us whatever we ask' (:35). Their request is an example of blatant self-centredness. Ronald Kernaghan (2007:203) detects 'a certain perversity in the way they approached Jesus.' He continues to explain that '[t]he terms of their request – that Jesus do whatever they asked – transgressed the normal relationship between teacher and pupil [...] It is as though they were asking Jesus to become their servant' (:203)' It seems that the two believed that there would be a kind of fight for the best places in God's kingdom, and so they thought it would be clever to make a kind of reservation. Their request, however, was an attempt to bend God's will to their will.

Like most of the Jewish people at that time, James and John had the wrong idea of the kingdom the Messiah would establish (cf. Hurtado 1998:171). They were hoping that Jesus would establish an earthly kingdom that would liberate Israel from their Roman oppressors. They were hoping that Jesus would establish a powerful kingdom that would demonstrate the superiority of the Jewish nation and their God. Obviously, James and John thought, as Jesus' disciples, they would get some position of power and influence in that new kingdom. 'David Garland 1996:411) suggests that they foresaw 'themselves as the elite of the elite, ruling over others in an earthly empire'. It is against this background that they asked him if they might sit on each side of king Jesus, 'Let one of us sit at your right and the other at your left in your glory' (:37). The two brothers envisioned 'their vocation on the traditional model of a power-wielding Christ', while Jesus lifts up his passion as a model for their ministry (Driggers 2007:69).

Jesus replies to his disciples by turning their value system upside down. They have asked to share in Jesus' glory, but all that Jesus can offer them is a share in his suffering, 'Can you drink the cup I drink or be baptised with the baptism I am baptised with? (:38)' The cup was a familiar Old Testament metaphor of God's wrath (e.g., Psalm 75:5, Isaiah 51:17, Jeremiah 49:12). It is mentioned again at the Last Supper (14:23-25) and in the prayer which Jesus prayed in the garden of Gethsemane (14:36). Likewise, *baptism* is a frequently used Old Testament image for death and divine judgement (Psalm 69:2, Psalm 124:4, Isaiah 43:2). English (1996:181) speaks of 'a violent image' which 'has about it the sense of being forcibly plunged beneath the waters, cast into the depths.' Jesus was going to Jerusalem to receive that kind of baptism. He was going there to bear the sins of the world. That was the cup he was given to drink. Whoever wanted to follow him would have to expect the same. As Kernaghan (2007:204-205) notes:

> In light of those texts the cup Jesus offered James and John was an invitation to share in his humiliation and death at the hands of the nations. The baptism and cup point beyond the impending confrontation between Jesus and the powers in Jerusalem to the disciples' subsequent confrontations with the nations.

Just as the question was posed to the sons of Zebedee, every follower of Christ is asked to share in his baptism and drink of his cup. Are we willing to do so? Will we be obedient even if it is going to cost us our lives?

Jesus leaves his disciples with no doubt that his kingdom is not of this world. It is not centred on palaces or thrones but in the hearts and lives of his followers. Jesus' kingdom is not about worldly power but service in the power of the Holy Spirit. In the words of Jesus:

> You know that those who are regarded as rulers of the Gentiles lord it over them, and their high officials exercise authority over them. Not so with you. Instead, whoever wants to become great among you must be your servant, and whoever wants to be first must be slave of all (10:42-44)

The two brothers wanted the highest positions in Jesus' kingdom, but Jesus told them that true greatness comes from serving others. Jesus' new community is organised on different principles to those of the world. In the world, people measure greatness by personal achievement and success, but in Jesus' kingdom serving others is the sign of true greatness. Instead of seeking to have our needs met, we need to look for ways in which we can minister to the needs of others.

Mark tells us about the brothers' claim that they could share Jesus' cup and baptism (10:39). Perhaps they shared some common Jewish beliefs and associated the cup Jesus had mentioned with the luxurious messianic meal and the baptism he had talked about with God's renewal of his people that would announce the coming of God's kingdom (English 1996:181-182). According to Garland 1996:412), their response, 'We can', demonstrates a high degree of self-confidence in their abilities. Garland continues: 'They believe they can endure a little hardship if Jesus will grant them seats of power and corner offices. They understand faithful discipleship to Jesus as a means to a selfish end; it will help them achieve their goal of having powers over others.' Jesus, however, is talking about suffering. He is talking about his suffering at the cross: 'You will drink the cup I drink and be baptised with the baptism I am baptised with' (:39). Interestingly, James and John wanted security, but Jesus is talking about the cost of discipleship. To follow Jesus would be costly for both; both would suffer for Jesus and his gospel. Ultimately, James died as a martyr (Acts 12:2) and John was forced to live in exile (Rev. 1:9).

In summary, James and John wanted honour, power and security, while Jesus offered them sacrifice, service and suffering. There are clearly two different ways to live. The first way is the way of the world, and the throne is a symbol of that way. For people who choose that way, it is ultimately all about themselves. The second way is the way of Jesus. It is the way of the cross on which Jesus gave his life as a ransom for many. For people who choose that way, it is ultimately all about Jesus and his kingdom. Edwards (2002:287) writes that Jesus' selfless service to others established a whole new sense of discipleship. The essence of discipleship has its origin in God's love. Jesus is the ultimate example of such discipleship, or as Ferguson (2002:174) puts it:

> But discipleship is also a 'modelling' process. It means being like Jesus! He came to serve others, not to be served by them. He came to give his life for others. If James and John and all the others really were going to be his disciples, then it was time they began to live like their Master.

Like the early disciples, we all are called to model our lives on him. Therefore, let us now consider how Jesus' model of discipleship can be beneficial to the Namibian Church today.

Chapter Five

Mark's Model of Discipleship and the Namibian Church

Throughout his gospel Mark shows us that certain elements are essential to Christian discipleship, such as self-denial, taking up the cross and following Christ. All these elements require the active participation of all who confess Jesus as the Messiah. Followers of Christ must 'lose their lives' to gain eternal life. Jesus' model of discipleship, as it is presented by Mark, involves sacrifice, suffering and service. This understanding of discipleship, however, is not unique to Mark's Gospel. Pointing to Romans 8:17, Harrington (2013:154) notes: 'Mark's understanding of discipleship was the same as that of Paul [...] His preoccupation with discipleship follows hard on his concern with Christology [..].' Harrington continues: 'For Mark there is no other way of discipleship. Following the path of the victory of Christ, the Christian is not preserved from suffering and even death but is sustained through suffering and death' (:154). Much of Mark's material resonates with Simba Musvamhiri's description of Christian discipleship. He writes:

> Discipleship is a long-term relationship with Jesus. Since a disciple embraces or should adhere to the teachings of Christ, this relationship continually builds trust, love [and] forgiveness. Discipleship should display spiritual growth, dying to self and living by the grace of God through faith in Christ [...] discipleship is a process where a person allows God to change their ungodly values into godly values. Discipleship is about relationships not programs [...] It is clear from the Scriptures that the disciple has no special privilege or power of his own. The main spring of his life is the strength that comes from his fellowship with Christ (2011:15-16).

Like Jesus, his disciples are called to a life of service. Jesus voluntarily became a servant to all and executed his service unto death because that was the will of God, or in the words of Peter Maiden (2014:50): 'Service was in the mind of Jesus as he approached the cross: the opportunity to serve his Father and humanity was at the forefront of his mind.' Herewith, Jesus demonstrated that discipleship means renouncing all self-interest and acting for the benefit of others. This has consequences for Christian leadership. Harrington's explanation is worth quoting in full:

> Mark has made the point that the revelation of Jesus cannot be acknowledged by one who is not ready to enter into the spirit of discipleship and thereby become "last" and "servant". One would hope that the Christian of today is attuned to the unambiguous message of this word of Jesus: greatness in his church is found in diakonia ("service"). A first step is to have discerned this. It is the right of the people of God to have such service. It is their right to demand that leadership in the Church, at every level, be service, not in word but in deed (2013:155-156).

Current Leadership Trends in the Namibian Church

Having been involved in Christian ministry in Namibia for almost 20 years, I have observed that there is a strong emphasis on leadership and at the same time a lack of discipleship in many churches. The understanding of church leadership, it seems, is strongly influenced by cultural values and practices and less so by biblical standards. Namibia is a collectivistic culture with a relatively high power distance. High-power-distance cultures 'assume a large status gap between those who have power and those who don't' (Plueddemann 2009:93). As a result, Namibian political, traditional and religious leaders are shown great respect and honour. For example, when a pastor visits a congregation in another part of the country church members will prepare an expensive meal and offer the pastor a comfortable bed to sleep in. Sometimes, they will book a guesthouse for him or her. In other cases, people do not feel comfortable accommodating visiting pastors at their houses because they believe that they are not worthy enough to do so. I remember preaching at a memorial service on a Friday evening. After the service, I walked home because I did not own a car at that time. I had just left the church when a car stopped next to me in the street. The driver told me that an elderly lady from the church had sent him to drive me home because the pastor should not have to walk.

It seems that in many Namibian churches such practices and their underlying values are not questioned by their leaders. Some simply accept them as given, while others encourage and foster them. Some even demand such preferential treatment. Put differently, instead of genuinely contextualising biblical leadership models, church leaders practice a culturally conditioned leadership. From my observation, Christian leadership in Namibia is seen as a high and honourable position that provides leaders with wealth, status and power. There is a common belief among Christians that material wealth and prestige go hand in hand with church leadership. Thus, many Christians expect their leaders to live in a wealthier neighbourhood and own expensive cars and Christian leaders are only too willing to meet these expectations. This is a phenomenon which can be observed in many parts of Africa. Tokunboh Adeyemo (2006:546) offers another helpful explanation when he writes:

> The introduction of a monetary economy and the modern military system challenged leadership derived from mystical powers. With the growth of new government structures, large corporations and elaborate infrastructure came demands for new forms of leadership. Unfortunately, some of the strengths and values of the old systems such as their emphasis on seasoned knowledge of life, wisdom, *ubuntu* and *ujamaa*, were discredited or lost and replaced with pride and arrogance. Leadership became focused on position, privileges, power and *pesa* ('money' in Swahili). By and large, leadership came to be understood in terms of a secular Western model. But this 'hand in the pocket' style of leadership is neither biblical nor African.

Prosperity gospel teaching, which is quite common, has contributed to such views and practices in Namibia. In his article *Namibian Churches and Funding: A Critical Introduction* Thorsten Prill (2020:6) observes:

> Namibian prosperity preachers are heavily influenced by Nigerian prosperity theology which 'shuns asceticism and seeks abundance in all areas of one's life'. In the mushrooming prosperity churches of Namibia giving in general and tithing in particular play indeed an important role. Referring to passages like Malachi 3:10, prosperity preachers not only tell their congregations that they are stealing from God by not tithing, they also challenge them to test God by giving more to him. Basilius Kasera, a systematic theologian and ethicist who teaches at the University of Namibia, speaks of the principle of a hundredfold return. This principle,

central to the militant form of the prosperity gospel, suggests the more money people give to God, the more money they will receive in return.

The results of such teaching can be seen not only in the expensive lifestyles of some church leaders but also in the life of the church. While many church members walk to church for the Sunday services many pastors enjoy a designated parking place next to the church entrance. In some independent churches, the church leaders have armour-bearers, special seats and even separate pastors' offerings. Leadership positions are exclusively filled by members of one or two families who claim ownership of the church. Leaders of such churches often hold that they are beyond criticism and demand total submission from their congregational members. Prill (2015:57) explains:

> They argue that they have been chosen by God to act and speak on his behalf. Therefore, they are not accountable to their churches for anything they say or do. As representatives of God on earth their power is absolute and must not be questioned, or so they think. The slightest criticism is silenced by pointing church members to passages such as Matthew 7:1 ('Do not judge, or you too will be judged') and Psalm 105:15 ('Do not touch my anointed ones; do my prophets no harm.').

Having said that, some of these attitudes and practices can also be observed in mainline denominations. Thus, some church members, especially older people, seem to worship the ground on which their leaders walk. They do not dare to correct their pastors or church elders even if it is apparent that the leaders are wrong. Likewise, church leaders expect to be treated like royalty at weddings and funerals. It is not unusual for them to be given seats at the high table and to be provided with the best dishes and cutlery. Many leaders insist that people always address them with their clerical titles, and people oblige because they fear the consequences of not using styles, such as reverend, bishop or apostle when speaking to the man or woman of God. Conrad Mbewe (2011), a Zambian Baptist theologian, strongly warns against such an attitude among church African church leaders. He writes:

> Pride is such a danger to church leadership [...] If you are not cultivating the grace of humility, church power will go to your head. You will begin to feel as if you "have arrived". Church activities will degenerate into a personal empire-building project. As the Lord blesses you further, you will begin to think you are the greatest thing to hit the world. You will fail to be a servant in the church and instead will feel like a chief executive officer. You will fail to listen to others, especially if they are only church members or pastors of smaller churches (:153-154)

Against this background, it is not surprising that the term *discipleship* is hardly used in many Namibian churches. However, when it is used, people seem to understand it as the process of training new church leaders but not as a relationship with Jesus which can be costly. They seem to ignore that Jesus has called his disciples, as Adeyemo (2006:1223) notes, to cross-bearing, self-denial and putting him first over all other relationships. He continues to explain:

> Faithful disciples are characterized by qualities such as abiding in Jesus' word, steadfast faith in him, loyalty to him, love for another, walking in the light, bearing fruit and humble service to one another [...] Discipleship also requires obedience to his commands [...], specially the commands to love God and our neighbours and to make disciples of all nations [...] (:1223).

One can only agree with Adeyemo when he writes that the New Testament concept of discipleship is rare today 'because of the teaching of cheap grace' and that abuse of the concept has led to the formation of Christian cults and the privatisation of the Christian faith in Africa (:1223).

Promoting Biblical Discipleship and Leadership

There is a lack of biblical discipleship and leadership in the Namibian church at large. If that is to change, the Namibian church must return to the Scriptures and rediscover the model of discipleship as we can find it presented by Mark and other biblical writers.

Firstly, Namibian church leaders need to understand that Christian leadership and discipleship cannot be separated from each other. Jesus was the leader of his disciples, and they were his followers. Everybody who confesses Jesus as the Messiah becomes his follower. Church leaders who confess Jesus as their Saviour are also disciples of Jesus and, therefore, ought to adopt his example of discipleship.

Secondly, Namibian Christians need to allow the New Testament teachings on discipleship to challenge their values and practices. Respect for older people and leaders, for example, is an important traditional African value (cf. Nkansah-Obrempong 2013:13). When people greet an older person or someone who is in authority, such as chiefs, teachers, politicians or religious leaders, they usually bow or bend their knees. In Namibia, there are also special counters for older people in banks and tills in supermarkets to make sure that they do not have to wait in long queues. To treat older people and leaders respectfully is something that Namibian children learn from an early age. However, it is problematic when church leaders openly or in more subtle ways demand such respect from their members and others. It is problematic when they stress the importance of respect because they enjoy their status in society so much or even see themselves as rulers who are not accountable to their flock. In his gospel Mark stresses that such a practice is unreconcilable with true Christian discipleship. In 10:42-43, he records the following words of Jesus: 'You know that those who are regarded as rulers of the Gentiles lord it over them, and their high officials exercise authority over them. Not so with you.' Such a practice reflects the ways of the world which have no place in Christ's church. The church and its leaders must be different, or in Jesus' words: 'Instead, whoever wants to become great among you must be your servant, and whoever wants to be first must be slave of all (:43-44).' What is required of true disciples, whether they occupy a leadership position or not, is humility, or as James Plueddemann (2009:102) writes:

> The Bible teaches respect for those in authority but also that those in authority must not demand to be held in high esteem. Leaders in high-power-distance cultures need to be aware of the dangers of pride in position and lording it over followers. Followers in low-power-distance cultures need to show proper respect for those in authority over them. Both leaders and followers are to clothe themselves with humility toward one another […]

Jesus' demonstration of leadership (or rather discipleship) brings a new perspective to Christian leaders (Mark 8:34-35; 9:35-37; 10:34-45). Jesus is the servant-leader of whom the prophet Isaiah speaks about in the so-called servant songs. Philip Greenslade (2002:111) notes:

> The servant leader is marked by a gentleness which makes him great. "A bruised reed he will not break, and a smouldering wick he will not snuff out" (Isa. 42:3). He is keen to encourage the weak and bolster the confidence of the timid. He will seek to impart faith and hope to the dispirited and to fan into flame potential gifts and abilities in others.

This is the kind of leadership Jesus wants to see in his church. Instead of asking people to serve their leaders, Jesus expects leaders to serve the people he has entrusted to them. A true leader is a servant leader, or as Mookgo Solomon Kgatle (2015:123) puts it: 'Servant leaders are those who combine leadership with servant-hood, because without service leadership becomes lordship and dictatorship.'

Thirdly, Namibian Christians need to allow the New Testament teachings on discipleship to challenge their theological views which have been influenced by prosperity teaching and other false ideas about Christian leadership. True disciple-ship and leadership are not about success, wealth and power but sacrifice and suffering (cf. Van Emmenes, Rousseau and Viljoen 2017). Mark leaves his readers in no doubt that being a disciple of Jesus is costly. It might involve, as Jesus warned the sons of Zebedee, drinking the cup that he drank and being baptised with the baptism that he was baptised with (cf. 10:38). Jesus clearly taught his followers the cost of discipleship, or as Greenslade (2002:120) writes:

> He spelt out to them what becoming a leader in His Church would involve. Unable to carry His unique cost, every potential leader must take up his own and learn to follow on a self-denying road. Never, as their ministry for Him took them across the Ancient World to their appointed martyrdoms or lonely Patmoses, would they ever be able to say He had disguised the cost.

Once Namibian church leaders see Jesus as the suffering servant of God and understand discipleship as displayed and taught by him in Mark's Gospel, hopefully, the desire for recognition, power and material wealth will fade and sacrificial service towards others will grow and become common practise in our churches. To facilitate such change Namibian churches should consider incorporating teaching sessions on discipleship not only into the training programmes for new church leaders, both lay and ordained, but also into catechism classes, congregational bible studies, home groups, etc. These teachings will help Namibian Christians to develop a spirit of servanthood, which is so manifest in the life and ministry of the ultimate servant, Jesus Christ, who came not to be served but to serve and to give his life as a ransom for many.

Bibliography

Adam, J.W. 2006, *The Performative Nature and Function of Isiah 40-55* (London: T & T Clark, 2006)

Adeyemo, T., 'Discipleship', in *Africa Bible Commentary*, ed. T. Adeyemo (Nairobi: Word Alive Publishers, 2006)

Adeyemo, T., 'Leadership', in *Africa Bible Commentary*, ed. T. Adeyemo (Nairobi: Word Alive Publishers, 2006)

Akin, D.L., *Exalting Jesus in Mark* (Nashville: Holman Reference, 2014)

Alexander, T.D., *The Servant King: The Bible's Portrait of the Messiah* (Leicester: IVP, 1998)

Alexander T.D., Rosner B.S., Carson D.A., Goldsworthy G. (eds), *New Dictionary of Biblical Theology* (Downers Grove: IVP, 2000)

Barnett, P., *The Servant King: Reading Mark Today* (Sydney: Aquila Press, 1991)

Barry, J.D., *The Resurrected Servant in Isaiah* (Colorado Springs: Paternoster Publishing, 2010)

Bauer, D.R., 'Son of God', in *Dictionary of Jesus and the Gospels*, eds. J.B. Green, S. McKnight and I.H. Marshall (Leicester, IVP, 1992)

Bellinger, W.H. and Farmer, W.R. (eds), *Jesus and the Suffering Servant: Isaiah 53 and Christian Origins* (Eugene: Wipf & Stock, 2009)

Black, C.C, *Mark* (Nashville: Abingdon Press, 2011)

Blomberg, C.L., *Jesus and the Gospels: An Introduction and Survey* (Nashville: Boardman & Holman Publishers, 1997)

Bock, D.L. and Glaser, M. (eds), *The Gospel According to Isaiah 53: Encountering the Suffering Servant in Jewish and Christian Theology* (Grand Rapids: Kregel, 2012)

Boring, M.E., *Mark: A Commentary* (Louisville: Westminster John Knox Press, 2006)

Brooks J.A., *Mark* (Nashville: Broadman & Holman, 1991)

Bultema, H., *Commentary on Isaiah* (Grand Rapids: Kregel, 1981)

Carson, D.A. and Moo, D.J., *An Introduction to the New Testament* (Grand Rapids: Zondervan, 2005)

Carson, D. and Beale, G., *Commentary on the New Testament Use of the Old Testament* (Grand Rapids: Michigan: Baker Academic, 2007)

Cole R.A, *The Gospel According to St Mark* (Leicester: IVP, 1989)

Cole, V.B., 'Mark', in *Africa Bible Commentary*, ed. T. Adeyemo (Nairobi: Word Alive Publishers, 2006)

Cranfield, C.E.B., *The Gospel According to St Mark* (Cambridge: Cambridge University Press, 1979)

Dickson N. K., 'Marks of True Christian Discipleship: Reflections from Mark 10:35-45'. *Research on Humanities and Social Sciences* 4 / 7 (2014):122-128.

Driggers, I. B., *Following God Through Mark: Theological Tension in the Second Gospel* (Louisville: Westminster John Know Press, 2007)

Dowd, S. and Malbon, E., 'The Significance of Jesus' Death in Mark: Narrative Context and Authorial Audience'. *Journal of Biblical Literature*, 2006 125(2), 271-297.

Dray, P., 2008, 'Isaiah 52:13-53:12: Isaiah on the Suffering Servant'. *Evangel* 26 / 2 (2008):33-36.

Edwards, J.R., *The Gospel According to Mark* (Grand Rapids: Eerdmans, 2002)

Ellen, D.L., 'Substitutionary Atonement and Cultic Terminology in Isaiah 53', in *The Gospel According to Isaiah 53: Encountering the Suffering Servant in Jewish and Christian Theology*, eds. D.L. Bock and M. Glaser, (Grand Rapids: Kregel, 2012)

English, D., *The Message of Mark* (Nottingham: IVP, 1992)

Estelle, B.D., 'The Exodus Motif in Isaiah', Westminster Seminary California, 2008. https://www.wscal.edu/resource-center/the-exodus-motif-in-isaiah; date of access: 06.07.2021.

Evans, C.A., *Mark 8:27-16:20, Volume 34B* (Nashville: Thomas Nelson, 2001)

Evans, C. A., 'Mark', in *New Dictionary of Biblical Theology,* eds. T.D. Alexander, B.S. Rosner, D.A. Carson and G. Goldsworthy (Downers Grove: IVP, 2000)

Farley, L.R., *The Gospel of Mark: The Suffering Servant* (Ben Lomond: Conciliar Press, 2004)

Farmer, R., 'Messiah/Christ', in *Lutterworth Dictionary of the Bible*, gen. ed. W.E. Mills (Cambridge: The Lutterworth Press, 1994)

France R.T., *The Gospel of Mark: A Commentary on the Greek Text* (Grand Rapids: Eerdmans, 2002)

France R T., 'The Servant of the Lord in the Teaching of Jesus'. *Tyndale Bulletin* 19 (1968):26-52.

Ferguson, S.B., *Let's Study Mark* (Edinburgh: Banner of Truth, 2002)

Garland, D.E. *Mark* (Grand Rapids: Zondervan, 1996)

Geisler, N.L., *A Popular Survey of the New Testament* (Grand Rapids: Baker Books, 2007)

Goldingay, J., *The Theology of the Book of Isaiah* (Downers Grove: IVP Academic, 2014)

Goldingay, J.E., *Daniel* (Dallas: Word Books, 1989)

Goldingay, J., *God's Prophet God's Servant: A Study in Jeremiah and Isaiah 40-55* (Exeter: Paternoster Press, 1984)

Grassmick J.D., 'Mark', in *The Bible Knowledge Commentary: An Exposition of the Scriptures*, eds. J.F. Walvoord and R.B. Zuck (Wheaton: Victor Books, 1985)

Greenslade, P., *Leadership: Reflections on Biblical Leadership Today* (Farnham: CWR, 2002)

Guntrie D., *New Testament Theology* (Downers Grove: IVP, 1981)

Hacking, P., *Isaiah: Crossway Bible Guide* (Leicester: Crossway Books, 2001)

Hafeman S.J. and House, P.R., *Central Themes in Biblical Theology, Mapping Unity in Diversity* (Nottingham: IVP, 2007)

Harrington, W.J., *Reading Mark for the First Time* (New York: Paulist Press, 2013)

Healy, M., *The Gospel of Mark* (Grand Rapids: Baker Academic, 2008)

Henderson, S.W., *Christology and Discipleship in the Gospel of Mark* (Cambridge: Cambridge University Press, 2006)

Hooker, M.D., *The Gospel According to Saint Mark* (London: Continuum, 1991)

Jackman, D., *Teaching Isaiah: Unlocking Isaiah for the Bible Teacher* (Fearn: Christian Focus, 2010)

Janowski, B. and Stuhlmacher, P. (eds), *The Suffering Servant: Isaiah 53 in Jewish and Christian Sources* (Grand Rapids: Eerdmans, 2004)

Kagema, D.N., 'Marks of True Christian Discipleship: Reflections from Mark 10:35-45'. *Research on Humanities and Social Sciences* 4/7 (2014)

Kaiser, W.C. jr., 'The Identity and Mission of the "Servant of The Lord", in *The Gospel According to Isaiah 53: Encountering the Suffering Servant in Jewish and Christian Theology*, eds. D.L. Bock and M. Glaser (Grand Rapids: Kregel, 2012)

Kasera, B.M., *The Biblical and Theological Examination of Prosperity Theology and its Impact among the Poor in Namibia*, unpublished MTh thesis (Sandton: South African Theological Seminary, 2012)

Keener, C.S. *The IVP Bible Background Commentary: New Testament.* (Downers Grove: IVP, 1993)

Kelhoffer, J.A. and McRay, J., 'Christ, Messiah, Anointed One', in *Evangelical Dictionary of Biblical Theology* (Grand Rapids: Baker Books, 1996)

Kernaghan, R.J., *Mark* (Nottingham: IVP, 2007)

Kgatle, M.S., *Servant Leadership in Mark 10:35-45 Applied to African Pentecostal Christianity*. Unpublished PhD dissertation (Pretoria: University of Pretoria, 2015)

Kingsbury, J.D., *The Christology of Mark's Gospel* (Philadelphia: Fortress Press, 1989)

Knight, G.A.F., *Servant Theology: A Commentary on the Book of Isaiah 40-55* (Edinburgh: Handsel Press, 1984)

Ladd, G.E., *A Theology of the New Testament*, (Grand Rapids: Eerdmans, 1974)

Lane, W.L., *The Gospel of Mark* (Grand Rapids: Eerdmans, 2010)

Le Peau, A.T., *Mark Through Old Testament Eyes: A Background and Application Commentary* (Grand Rapids: Kregel, 2017)

Le Roux, E., *Ethics in 1 Peter: The Imitatio Christi and the Ethics of Suffering in 1 Peter and the Gospel of Mark – A Comparative Study* (Eugene: Pickwick, 2018)

Lewis, P., *The Glory of Christ* (Carlisle: Paternoster, 2004)

MacLeod, D., *The Suffering Servant of the Lord: A Prophecy of Jesus Christ: An Exposition of Isaiah 52:13-53:12* (Eugene: Wipf & Stock, 2016)

Maiden, P., *Discipleship* (Hyderabad: Authentic Boos, 2014)

Markusse, G., *Salvation in the Gospel of Mark: The Death of Jesus and the Path of Discipleship* (Eugene: Pickwick, 2018)

Marshall, I.H., 'Son of Man', in: *Dictionary of Jesus and The Gospels*, eds. J.B. Green, S. McKnight and I.H. Marshall (Leicester: IVP, 1992).

Marshall, I.H., 'Jesus Christ', in *New Dictionary of Biblical Theology,* eds. T.D. Alexander T.D., B.S. Rosner, D.A. Carson and G. Goldsworthy (Downers Grove: IVP, 2000)

Marshall, I. H., *New Testament Theology* (Downers Grove: IVP, 2004)

Marshall, I. H., *A Concise New Testament Theology*, (Downers Grove: IVP, 2008)

Martin J.A, 'Isaiah', in *The Bible Knowledge Commentary: An Exposition of the Scriptures*, eds. J.F. Walvoord and R.B. Zuck (Wheaton: Victor Books, 1985)

Mbewe, C., *Foundations of the Flock: Truths About the Church for All the Saints* (Hannibal: Granted Ministries Press, 2011)

McKenna, M., *On Your Mark: Reading Mark in the Shadow of the Cross* (Maryknoll: Orbis Books, 2006)

Myers, C., 'Mark's Gospel: Invitation to Discipleship', in *The New Testament: Introducing the Way of Discipleship*, eds. W. Howard-Brook and S.H. Ringe (New York: Orbis Books, 2002)

Milne, B., *Know the Truth: A Handbook of Christian Belief* (Downers Grove: IVP, 2009)

Motyer, A.J., *The Prophecy of Isaiah* (Leicester: IVP, 1999a)

Motyer, A.J., *Isaiah* (Leicester: IVP, 1999b)

Nkansah-Obrempong, J., *Foundations for African Theological Ethics* (Carlisle: Langham Monographs, 2013)

Ortlund, R. jr., *Isaiah: God Saves Sinners* (Wheaton: Crossway, 2005)

Osei-Mensah, G., *Wanted Servant Leaders: The Challenge of Christian Leadership in Africa Today* (Accra: African Christian Press, 1990)

Oswalt, J.N., *Isaiah 40-66, New International Commentary on the Old Testament* (Grand Rapids: Eerdmans, 1998)

Page, S., 'Ransom Saying', in *Dictionary of Jesus and the Gospels*, ed. J.B. Green and S. McKnight (Leicester: IVP, 1992)

Pitre, B.J., *Jesus, the Tribulation, and the End of Exile: Restoration Eschatology and the Origins of Atonement* (Tübingen: Mohr Siebeck, 2005)

Pitre, B., 'The "Ransom for Many," the New Exodus, and the End of the Exile Redemption as the Restoration of All Israel (Mark 10:35-45)'. *Letter & Spirit* 1 (2005):41-68.

Placher, W., *Mark* (Louisville: Westminster John Knox, 2010)

Plueddemann, J.E., *Leading Across Cultures: Effective Ministry and Mission in the Global Church* (Downers Grove: IVP Academic, 2009)

Prill, T., 'Namibian Churches and Funding: A Critical Introduction', in *The Namibian Church and Money: A Biblical Perspective*, eds. T. Prill and J. van Wyk (München: Grin, 2020)

Prill, T., *Contemporary Issues in Mission: What Christians Need to Know* (München: Grin, 2015).

Rugwiji, T., 'The Salvific Task of the Suffering Servant in Isaiah 42:1-7: A Contemporary Perspective'. *Journal for Semitics* 23 / 2 (2014):289-314.

Ryle, J.C., *Expository Thoughts on Mark*, (Edinburgh: Banner of Trust, 1994)

Sadi, F., *A Study of Current Leadership Styles in the North African Church* (Carlisle: Langham Monographs, 2013)

Sabin, M.N., *The Gospel According to Mark* (Collegeville: Liturgical Press, 2005)

Schweizer, E., *The Good News According to Mark* (Southampton: The Camelot Press, 1970)

Smith, G., *Isaiah 40-66* (Nashville, Boardman & Holman Publishers, 2009)

Smuts, P. W., *Mark by the Book: A New Multidirectional Method for Understanding the Synoptic Gospels* (New Jersey: P&R Publishing, 2013)

Stein, R.H., *Mark* (Grand Rapids: Baker Academic, 2008)

Tan, K.H., *Mark: A New Covenant Commentary* (Cambridge: Lutterworth Press, 2016)

Telford W.R., *The Theology of the Gospel of Mark* (Cambridge: Cambridge University Press, 2002)

Thielman, F.S., 'The Atonement', in *Central Themes in Biblical Theology: Mapping Unity in Diversity*, eds. S.J. Hafemann and P.R. House Leicester: IVP, 2007)

Van Emmenes, G.C., Rousseau, P.A. and Viljoen, F.P., 'Christen-dissipelskap in die Markusevangelie as *critique* op die welvaartteologie'. *In die Skriflig / In Luce Verbi* (online) 51 / 1 (2017). http://www.scielo.org.za/pdf/ids/v51n1/04.pdf; Date of access: 13.9.2021.

Walton, J.H., Matthews, V.H. and Chavalas, M.W. (ed), *The IVP Bible Background Commentary: Old Testament* (Downers Grove: IVP, 2000)

Walton, J.H., 'The Imagery of the substitute King Ritual in Isaiah's Fourth Servant Song'. *Journal of Biblical Literature* 122/4 (2003):734-743.

Watts, R.E., 'Mark', in *Commentary on the New Testament Use of the Old Testament*, eds. G.K. Beale and D.A. Carson (Nottingham: Apollos, 2007)

Webb, B., *The Message of Isaiah* (Leicester: IVP, 1996)

Wessel, W., 'Mark', in *The Expositor's Bible Commentary, Volume 8*, gen. ed. F.E. Gaebelein (Grand Rapids: Regency, 1984)

Williams, D.W. and Noel, J., *Conversations with a Suffering Servant* (London: T&T Clark, 2021)

Williamson, L. jr., *Mark* (Louisville: Westminster John Knox Press, 2009)

Witherington III, B., *The Gospel of Mark: A Socio-Rhetorical Commentary* (Grand Rapids: Eerdmans, 2001)

Wolf, H.M., 'Isaiah', *Baker Encyclopaedia of the Bible* (Grand Rapids: Baker Book House, 1998).

Wolf, H.M., *Interpreting Isaiah: The Suffering and Glory of the Messiah* (Grand Rapids: Academie Books, 1985)

Wright, C. J. H., *Knowing Jesus through the Old Testament* (Oxford: Monarch Books, 2005)

Young, E.J., *The Book of Isaiah* (Grand Rapids: Eerdmans, 1972)

About the Author

Misseline Gordon is an ordained minister of the Rynse Kerk in Namibië (Rhenish Church in Namibia) serving as a lecturer at Namibia Evangelical Theological Seminary (NETS). She graduated from NETS with a Bachelor of Theology in 2002 and with a Bachelor Honours in Theology in 2017. From 2004 to 2017 she served in the Tsumeb Congregation of the Rhenish Church in both full-time and part-time capacities. Misseline Gordon is currently undertaking further postgraduate studies at London School of Theology.

Namibian Theological Research Papers (NTRP)

Volume 1
Themes in African Church History: Missionary Motives, Merits and Mistakes (2019)
Anthony Brendell & Thorsten Prill

Volume 2
The Namibian Church and Money: A Biblical Perspective (2020)
Johann van Wyk & Thorsten Prill

Volume 3
The Kingdom of God and the Christian Community in Rehoboth: The Sermon on the Mount and its Relevance for the Namibian Church (2021)
Heinz Mouton

Volume 4
Jesus, the Suffering Servant of Mark and Isaiah: A Role Model for Christian Discipleship in the Namibian Church (2021)
Misseline Gordon

Editor: Dr Thorsten Prill

Contact:
Edinburgh Bible College (EBC)
39 Greendykes Road
Broxburn EH52 5AF
Scotland
thorsten@edinburghbiblecollege.co.uk